U.S. Department of Justice
Office Justice Programs
National Institute of Justice

Walk-Through Metal Detectors for Use in Concealed Weapon and Contraband Detection

NIJ Standard–0601.02
Supersedes NIJ Standard–0601.01 dated September 2000
Supersedes NILECJ–STD–0601.00 dated October 1974

Nicholas G. Paulter, Jr.
Electricity Division
National Institute of Standards and Technology
Gaithersburg, MD 20899

Prepared for:
National Institute of Justice
Office of Science and Technology
Washington, DC 20531

January 2003

NCJ 193510

National Institute of Justice

Sarah V. Hart
Director

This standard was prepared for the National Institute of Justice, U.S. Department of Justice, by the Office of Law Enforcement Standards of the National Institute of Standards and Technology under Interagency Agreement 99–IJ–R–094, Project No. 02-002.

The NIJ Standard–0601.02, "Walk-Through Metal Detectors for Use in Concealed Weapon and Contraband Detection," is a revision to and supersedes the NIJ Standard-0601.01 published in September 2000. The 2000 revision addressed concerns of the criminal justice and public safety communities for an updated performance standard based on current technologies and responded to recommendations from the Law Enforcement and Corrections Technology Advisory Council. This current revision responds to comments received from industry and the criminal justice and public safety communities on the 2000 revision.

K.D. Rice of the Office of Law Enforcement Standards (OLES) of NIST and D.R. Larson of NIST are acknowledged for their comments and recommendations.

FOREWORD

The Office of Law Enforcement Standards (OLES) of the National Institute of Standards and Technology (NIST) provides technical support to the National Institute of Justice (NIJ) program to support law enforcement and criminal justice in the United States. OLES's function is to develop standards and conduct research that will assist law enforcement and criminal justice agencies.

OLES is: (1) subjecting existing equipment to laboratory testing and evaluation, and (2) conducting research leading to the development of several series of documents, including national standards, user guides, and technical reports.

This document covers research conducted by OLES under the sponsorship of NIJ. Additional reports as well as other documents are being issued under the OLES program in the areas of protective clothing and equipment, communications systems, emergency equipment, investigative aids, security systems, vehicles, weapons, and analytical techniques and standard reference materials used by the forensic community.

Technical comments and suggestions about this guide are welcome and may be addressed to the Office of Law Enforcement Standards, National Institute of Standards and Technology, 100 Bureau Drive, Stop 8102, Gaithersburg, MD 20899–8102.

Sarah V. Hart, Director
National Institute of Justice

CONTENTS

Page

FOREWORD iii
COMMONLY USED SYMBOLS AND ABBREVIATIONS vii
1. INTRODUCTION 1
   1.1 Purpose of the Standard 1
   1.2 Definitions 1
2. REQUIREMENTS FOR ACCEPTANCE 7
   2.1 Safety Specifications and Requirements 7
   2.2 Electrical Requirements 8
   2.3 Detection Performance Specifications 9
   2.4 Operating Requirements 11
   2.5 Mechanical Specifications and Requirements 15
   2.6 Functional Requirements 16
   2.7 Detector Mount 18
   2.8 Quality Control and Assurance 21
   2.9 Documentation 21
3. PERFORMANCE TESTING PROCEDURES 23
   3.1 General Test Conditions 23
   3.2 Detection Performance Tests 24
   3.3 Alarm Indication Test 32
   3.4 Test for Operation Near a Metal Wall, Steel Reinforced Floor, or Moving Metal Door 32
   3.5 Burn-In Test 34
4. FIELD TESTING PROCEDURES 34
   4.1 Large Object Size 34
   4.2 Medium Object Size 35
   4.3 Small Object Size 35
5. TEST OBJECTS DESCRIPTION 35
   5.1 Large Object Size Test Objects 35
   5.2 Medium Object Size Test Objects 38
   5.3 Small Object Size Test Objects 40
   5.4 Innocuous Item Test Objects 46
6. COMPLIANCE TEST REPORT FORM 53
7. REFERENCES 53

FIGURES

Figure 1. Diagram of walk-through metal detector showing the detector plane, the detector axis, and the x, y, and z axes of the measurement coordinate system 3

Figure 2. Diagram showing the detector and the detector mount, the detector plane, the detector floor, and the reference surface 4

Figure 3. Diagram illustrating the nine test measurement locations positioned in relation to the x and z axes of the measurement coordinate system 7

Figure 4. Test measurement locations for detection performance tests where the outer box represents the inside dimensions of the walk-through metal detector 10

Figure 5. Drawing of the detector mount showing the positioning of grooves for the steel reinforced floor test 19

Figure 6. Mechanical drawing of the reference surface 20

Figure 7. Drawing of assembly of items A, B, and C of test-object support platform 30

Figure 8. Drawing of assembly of items D and E of test-object support platform 31

COMMONLY USED SYMBOLS AND ABBREVIATIONS

A	ampere	H	henry	nm	nanometer
ac	alternating current	h	hour	No.	number
AM	amplitude modulation	hf	high frequency	o.d.	outside diameter
cd	candela	Hz	hertz (c/s)	Ω	ohm
cm	centimeter	i.d.	inside diameter	p.	page
CP	chemically pure	in	inch	Pa	pascal
c/s	cycle per second	IR	infrared	pe	probable error
d	day	J	joule	pp.	pages
dB	decibel	L	lambert	ppm	parts per million
dc	direct current	L	liter	qt	quart
°C	degree Celsius	lb	pound	rad	radian
°F	degree Fahrenheit	lbf	pound-force	rf	radio frequency
dia	diameter	lbf·in	pound-force inch	rh	relative humidity
emf	electromotive force	lm	lumen	s	second
eq	equation	ln	logarithm (base e)	SD	standard deviation
F	farad	log	logarithm (base 10)	sec.	section
fc	footcandle	M	molar	SWR	standing wave ratio
fig.	figure	m	meter	uhf	ultrahigh frequency
FM	frequency modulation	min	minute	UV	ultraviolet
ft	foot	mm	millimeter	V	volt
ft/s	foot per second	mph	miles per hour	vhf	very high frequency
g	acceleration	m/s	meter per second	W	watt
g	gram	N	newton	λ	wavelength
gr	grain	N·m	newton meter	wt	weight

area=unit^2 (e.g., ft^2, in^2, etc.); volume=unit^3 (e.g., ft^3, m^3, etc.)

PREFIXES

d	deci (10^{-1})	da	deka (10)
c	centi (10^{-2})	h	hecto (10^2)
m	milli (10^{-3})	k	kilo (10^3)
μ	micro (10^{-6})	M	mega (10^6)
n	nano (10^{-9})	G	giga (10^9)
p	pico (10^{-12})	T	tera (10^{12})

COMMON CONVERSIONS (See ASTM E380)

0.30480 m = 1 ft   4.448222 N = 1 lbf
25.4 mm = 1 in   1.355818 J = 1 ft·lbf
0.4535924 kg = 1 lb   0.1129848 N·m = 1 lbf·in
0.06479891 g = 1 gr   14.59390 N/m = 1 lbf/ft
0.9463529 L = 1 qt   6894.757 Pa = 1 lbf/in^2
3600000 J = 1 kW·hr   1.609344 km/h = 1 mph

Temperature: $T_{°C} = (T_{°F} - 32) \times 5/9$
Temperature: $T_{°F} = (T_{°C} \times 9/5) + 32$

NIJ Standard–0601.02

NIJ STANDARD FOR WALK-THROUGH METAL DETECTORS FOR USE IN CONCEALED WEAPON AND CONTRABAND DETECTION

1. INTRODUCTION

1.1 Purpose of the Standard

The purpose of this document is to establish performance requirements and testing methods for active walk-through metal detectors used to find metal weapons and/or metal contraband carried on a person and/or concealed by a nonmetal object.

1.2 Definitions

The definitions are provided to help the reader use and understand this document, which describes methods for evaluating active walk-through metal detectors used as weapons detectors. Terms that are defined here appear in *italics* in the remainder of this document.

All measurement units used in this document are metric. Length units are abbreviated: meter (m), centimeter (cm), and millimeter (mm). Where useful, English units are indicated in parentheses immediately following the metric units, such as "2.54 cm (1 in)."

1.2.1 Alarm Indication

A signal to warn of the detection of a metal object. The indication can be visual and/or auditory.

1.2.1.1 Positive Alarm Indication

The change in the *alarm indication* that corresponds to the detection of a metal object. Typically, the *alarm indication* is off until a metal object is detected.

1.2.1.2 Proportional Alarm Indication

An *alarm indication* proportional to the size, proximity, orientation, and material of an object.

1.2.2 Alarm Indicator

The device used to generate the *alarm indication*. For a visual indication, the alarm generating device can be a light bulb, lamp, light emitting diode, etc. For an auditory indication, the alarm generating device can be a horn, siren, buzzer, or similar item.

1.2.3 Active Detector

An *active detector* is generally a device that generates energy for illuminating the portal region of the detector. For the walk-through metal detector, the generated energy is in the form of a magnetic field. The interaction of the generated magnetic field with certain types of objects in the portal region of the detector and the ability to detect this interaction is the basis of operation for walk-through metal detectors.

1.2.4 Clean Tester

A person who does not carry any electrically conductive and magnetizable objects such as metallic belt buckles, metal buttons, cardiac pacemaker, coins, metal-frame eyeglasses, hearing aid, jewelry, keys, pens and pencils, shoes with metal arches or supports, metallic surgical implants, undergarment support metal, metal zippers, and similar items, which would significantly alter the signal produced when the person carries a *test object*.

1.2.5 Detection

The discovery or finding of a metallic object. The detection of a metallic object is transmitted to the operator by some type of *alarm indicator,* typically a visual or audible indicator.

1.2.6 Detector Axis

An imaginary line passing through and perpendicular to the *detector plane* that is centered vertically and horizontally within the portal of the walk-through metal detector and points in the direction of the subject's motion through the portal. See figure 1.

1.2.7 Detector Floor

The bottom plane of the detector portal.

1.2.8 Detector Mount

A nonconductive, nonmagnetic platform on which the walk-through metal detector rests. The *detector mount* locates the *detector floor* at a height of 32.5 cm (12.8 in) and contains grooves at 10 cm (4 in) below its top surface to facilitate the metal floor test required under section 3.4.2. The

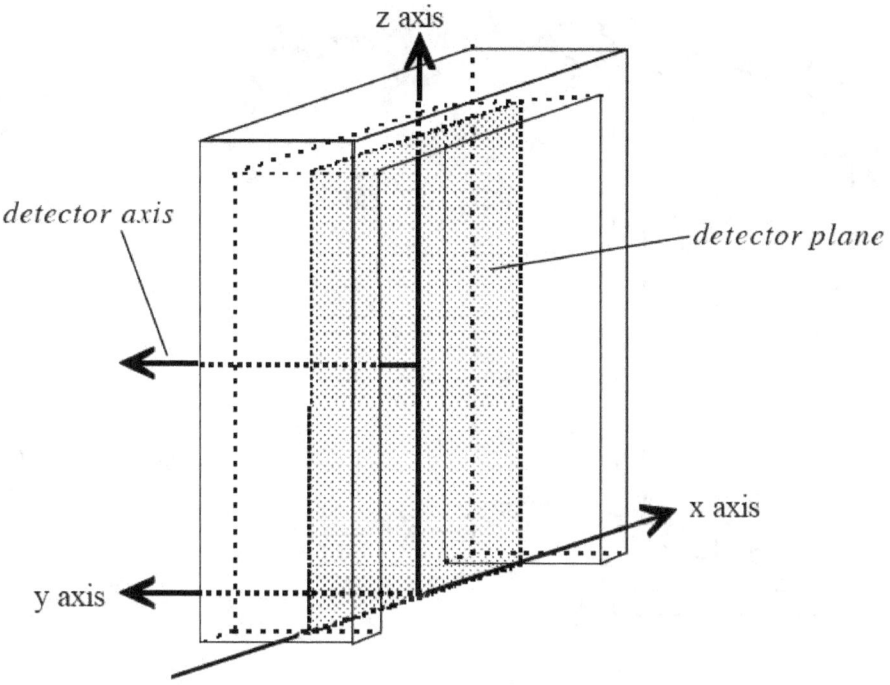

Figure 1. Diagram of walk-through metal detector showing the detector plane, the detector axis, and the x, y, and z axes of the measurement coordinate system

reference surface of the *detector mount* is parallel to the *detector plane*, contains tapped holes that mate to the mounting holes of the positioning system (see sec. 3.2.2.2), and holds the *detector plane* 0.5 m (1.7 ft) from the *reference surface*. The *detector mount* is supplied by the manufacturer and attached to the *detector positioner* at their *reference surfaces*. See figure 2.

1.2.9 Detector Plane

An imaginary plane (two-dimensional surface) that is parallel to the portal of the walk-through metal detector and that bisects the sensor region into two symmetric halves. The *detector plane* contains two orthogonal axes labeled the "x" axis and the "z" axis. See figure 1.

1.2.10 Detector Positioner

A nonconductive, nonmagnetic device that fixes the position of the *detector plane* and *detector axis* with respect to the *three-axes translation system*. The *detector positioner* includes a *reference surface* for attaching the *detector mount*. The *detector positioner* also includes a surface for attachment to the *three-axes translation system*.

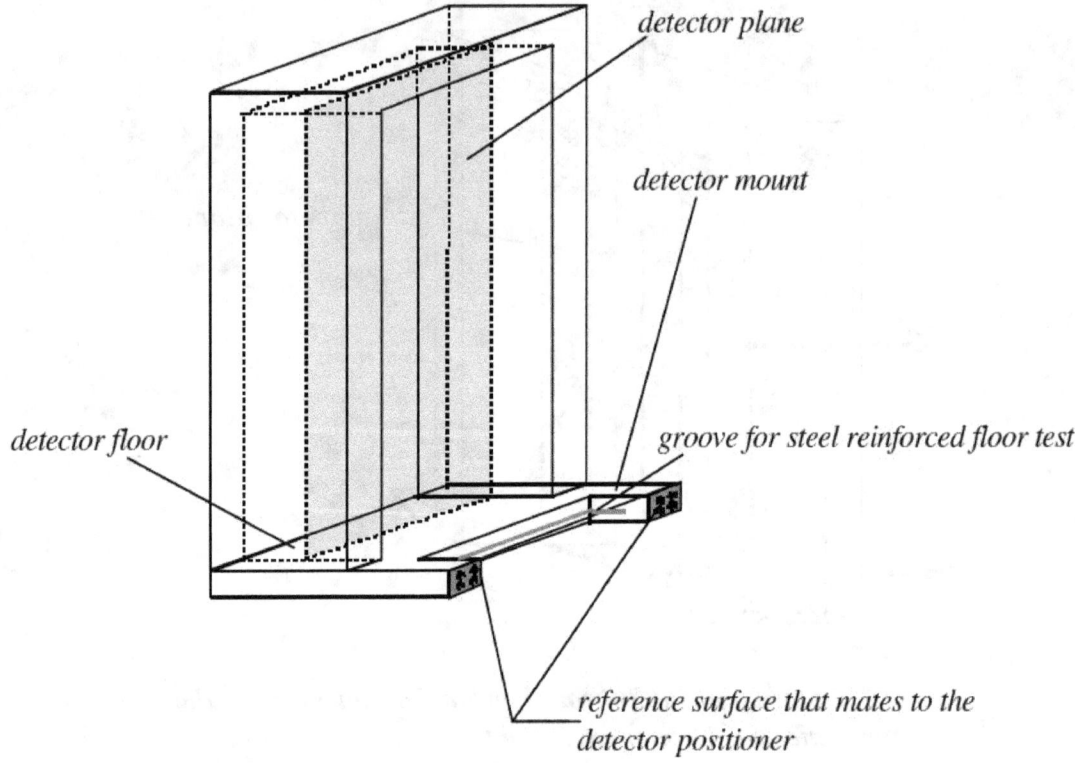

Figure 2. Diagram showing the detector and the detector mount, the detector plane, the detector floor, and the reference surface

1.2.11 Detector Response

The electrical signal generated by the sensor or sensor circuit of the detector and caused by an object interacting with the magnetic field generated by the detector. The *detector response* is the basis on which an *alarm indication* is derived.

1.2.12 Ground Surface

The surface on which the walk-through detector rests.

1.2.13 Measurement Coordinate System

A mutually orthogonal three-dimensional Cartesian coordinate system referenced to the *detector axis* and the *detector plane*. The three axes are labeled "x," "y," and "z," where the y axis is parallel to the *detector axis* and the x and z axes are in the *detector plane*. The orientation of the *test objects* and direction of the magnetic field is referenced to the *measurement coordinate system*. See figure 1.

1.2.14 Object Size Classes

A classification method based on the ability to detect metal objects of a minimum size. A detector may meet the requirements for one, two, or three *object size classes*, as defined below.

1.2.14.1 Large Object Size

The ability to detect handguns concealed on an individual that are constructed of either ferromagnetic or nonferromagnetic metal.

1.2.14.2 Medium Object Size

The ability to detect knives on an individual that are constructed of either ferromagnetic or nonferromagnetic metal. Large knives are defined for this purpose as knives with blade lengths exceeding 7.5 cm (3 in).

1.2.14.3 Small Object Size

The ability to detect small weapons and contraband items concealed on an individual that are constructed of either ferromagnetic or nonferromagnetic metal. Small weapons and contraband items are defined as items that can be used to injure another person or to defeat security devices.

1.2.15 Reference Surface

The planes located on the *detector mount* and *detector positioner* used to attach the *detector mount* and *detector positioner*. See figure 2.

1.2.16 Specific Test Measurement Location

The nine positions in the x-z plane (the x-z plane is parallel to the *detector plane*) through which the *test object(s)* shall be passed. The *test measurement locations* are based on the size of the average male person and are defined at points along the x and z axes of the *measurement coordinate system*. There are two locations at ankle height separated approximately by hip width, two at hip height separated approximately by hip width, two at shoulder height separated approximately by torso width, one at top of head height centered along the z axis, one at slightly below armpit height centered along the z axis, and one at crotch height centered along the z axis. See figure 3.

1.2.17 Test Object

An item used to test the walk-through detection performance. The *test object* is an encased replica of a metallic item that is either a weapon, can be used as a weapon, or can be used to defeat security devices. The shape of the encasement is a parallelepiped. The encasement has up to 12 holes that allow the replica to be oriented with respect to the *measurement coordinate system*; no more than nine possible orientations are allowed, one to three orientations for each unique orthogonal surface, but no more than three, of the parallelepiped.

1.2.17.1 Large Object Size Test Objects

Test objects that are used to test the *large object size* detection performance of walk-through metal detectors used as weapon detectors. Mechanical drawings of the *large object size test objects* are provided in section 5.1.

1.2.17.2 Medium Object Size Test Objects

Test objects that are used to test the *medium object size* detection performance of walk-through metal detectors used as weapon detectors. Mechanical drawings of the *medium object size test objects* are provided in section 5.2.

1.2.17.3 Small Object Size Test Objects

Test objects that are used to test the *small object size* detection performance of walk-through metal detectors used as weapon detectors. Mechanical drawings of the *small object size test objects* are provided in section 5.3.

1.2.17.4 Innocuous Item Test Objects

Test objects that are used to test the discrimination performance of the *large object size* and *medium object size* walk-through metal detectors. Mechanical drawings of the *innocuous item test objects* are provided in section 5.4.

1.2.18 Test Object Axes

The three mutually orthogonal axes of the *test object* that are referenced to and have a one-to-one correspondence to the axes of the *measurement coordinate system*.

1.2.19 Test Measurement Grid Location

The positions in the x-z plane (the x-z plane is parallel to the *detector plane*) through which the *test object(s)* shall be passed. The *test measurement grid locations* are located within the rectangular region bounded by the extrema of the *specific test measurement locations* (± 20 cm ± 0.1 cm for the x axis and 5 cm and 180 cm for the z axis) and are located on a 5 cm ± 0.1 cm by 5 cm ± 0.1 cm grid.

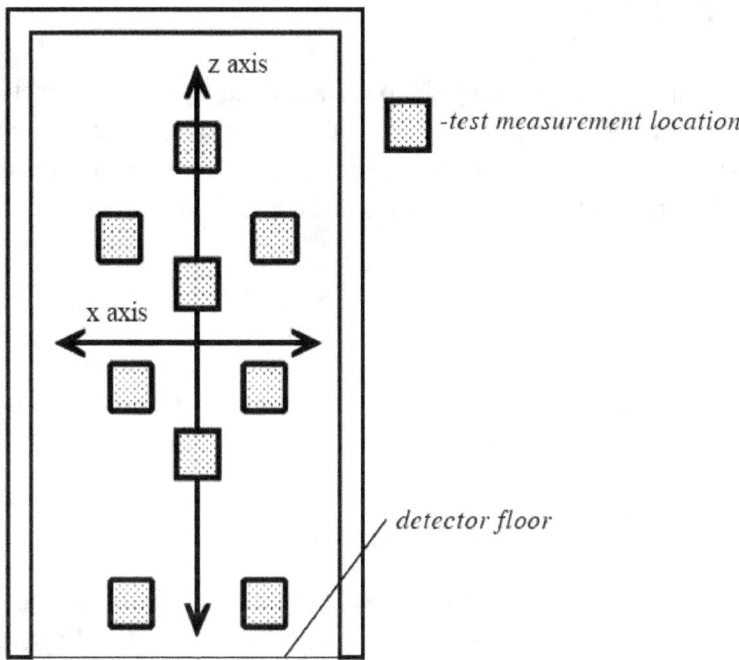

Figure 3. Diagram illustrating the nine test measurement locations positioned in relation to the x and z axes of the measurement coordinate system

1.2.20 Three-Axes Positioning System

Also known as a Cartesian robot, the *three-axes positioning system* provides three mutually orthogonal directions of linear translation. The *three-axes positioning system* is used to place *test objects* in the magnetic field of the detector.

2. REQUIREMENTS FOR ACCEPTANCE

The detector shall meet the requirements and specifications stated in this section. Reports shall be provided on the Compliance Test Report forms mentioned in section 6.

2.1 Safety Specifications and Requirements

2.1.1 Electrical

The detector shall comply with UL 60950, *Safety for Information Technology Equipment*, if the electrical potential difference between any two points within the detector is greater than 30 V rms (42.4 V peak-to-peak) for alternating currents (ac) or greater than 60 V referenced to ground for direct currents (dc).

2.1.2 Mechanical

The detector shall not expose (1) any sharp corners or edges that can puncture, cut, or tear the skin or clothing or injure persons coming in contact with the detector, (2) external wires, connectors, and cables, except the power cable described in section 2.2.2, or (3) loose covers and cowlings. The minimum exposed radius of curvature for corners and edges shall be 1 mm (0.04 in).

2.1.3 Exposure

The level of the magnetic field generated by the detector shall be less than the exposure limits specified in ACGIH–0302 (1996), *Sub-Radio Frequency (30 kHz and below) Magnetic Fields*, as amended.

2.1.4 Personal Medical Electronic Devices

The magnetic fields produced by the detector shall not generate voltages across the leads of the test probe specified in *Safety Code, Recommended Safety Procedures for the Selection, Installation and Use of Active Metal Detectors (the Safety Procedures)*, Radiation Protection Bureau, Canadian Minister of National Health and Welfare that exceed the maximum permitted probe output specified in the Safety Procedures when tested in accordance to the Safety Procedures.

2.2 Electrical Requirements

2.2.1 AC Power

The detector shall operate at the available power line voltages with variations in line voltage less than or equal $\pm$ 10 % of the nominal value and with variations in frequency $\leq \pm$ 5 % of the nominal value. The manufacturer shall provide an indicator to alert the operator of the ac power status, if outside of range, as described in section 2.6.2.5.

2.2.2 AC Connector

An ac power connector socket shall be provided on both sides of the detector portal unless the operation and function of the detector is the same for traffic flow in both directions, in which case an ac connector is required on one side of the portal. To provide a secure connection, the ac connector socket shall not be exposed.

2.3 Detection Performance Specifications

The detection performance specifications shall be tested using the specific set of detector program parameter settings that is specified by the manufacturer to be appropriate for each *object size class* of detector that is to be tested.

2.3.1 Detection Sensitivity

The *detector response* shall be measured at all *specific test measurement locations* and *test measurement grid locations* and shall provide a *positive alarm indication* for each *test object* of the appropriate *object size class* for each allowed orientation of the *test object axes* with respect to the *measurement coordinate system* moving at a speed of 1.0 m/s ± 0.05 m/s in accordance with section 3.2.3. The results shall be recorded and a report shall be provided. The *test object*, the orientation of the *test object axes* of this *test object* with respect to the *measurement coordinate system*, and the *test measurement location* (see fig. 4) of this *test object* that provide a minimum *detector response* for the appropriate *object size class* shall be recorded and specified as the "minimum detection conditions." The *test object*, the orientation of the *test object axes* of this *test object* with respect to the *measurement coordinate system*, and the x- and y-axes scan positions (see sec. 3.2.3) of the *test measurement grid locations* that provide a minimum *detector response* for the appropriate *object size class* shall be recorded and specified as the "alternate minimum detection conditions." If more than one x-z position can satisfy the requirements of the minimum detection condition or the alternate minimum detection condition, then one position shall be selected for each condition.

2.3.2 Speed

The detector shall provide a *positive alarm indication* for the "minimum detection conditions" and "alternate minimum detection conditions" for each appropriate *object size class* as determined according to section 2.3.1 for the *test object* moving at the following speeds: 0.2 m/s ± 0.01 m/s, 0.5 m/s ± 0.01 m/s, 1.0 m/s ± 0.01 m/s, and 2.0 m/s ± 0.01 m/s as tested in accordance with section 3.2.4. The results shall be recorded.

2.3.3 Repeatability

The detector shall provide a *positive alarm indication* without failure for the "minimum detection conditions" and "alternate minimum detection conditions" for each appropriate *object size class* as determined according to section 2.3.1 for the *test object* moving at a speed of 1.0 m/s ± 0.05 m/s for 50 consecutive trials under the following conditions:

a. The delay between subsequent trials of a given *test object* shall be no more than 5 s.
b. The detector sensitivity shall not be readjusted between trials of a given *test object* or between trials of the *test objects* of a given *object size class*.

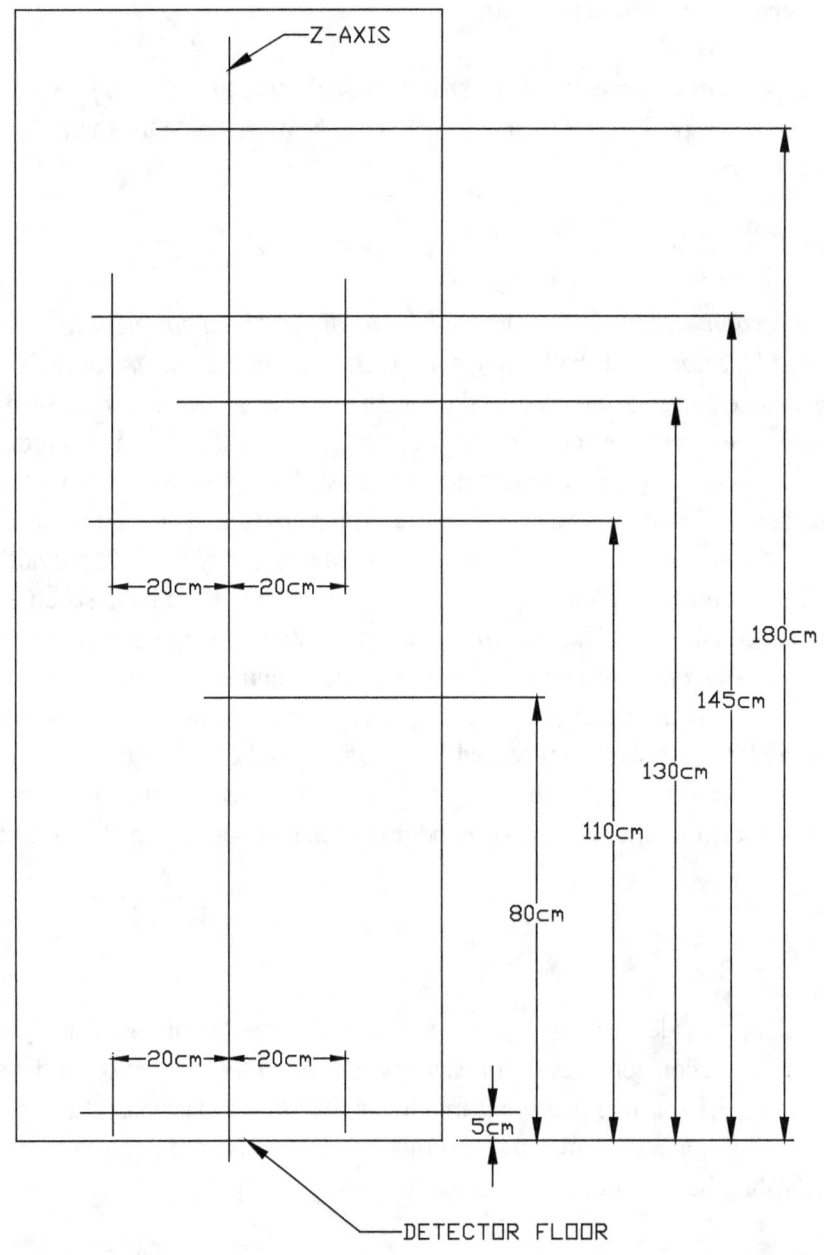

Figure 4. Test measurement locations for detection performance tests where the outer box represents the inside dimensions of the walk-through metal detector

This test shall be performed according to section 3.2.4, and the results shall be recorded. The results of this test can also be called the probability of detection, p_d, with a required p_d of 1.00 (or 100 %).

2.3.4 Discrimination

The detector shall meet the requirements of section 2.3.1 and without readjustment shall not provide a *positive alarm indication* for at least 20 of 25 consecutive trials when tested in accordance with section 3.2.5 for the *innocuous item test object*s moving at a speed of 1.0 m/s ± 0.1 m/s, and the results shall be recorded. The results of this test can also be called the probability of false alarm, p_{fa}, with a required p_{fa} of less than 0.2 (or 20 %).

2.3.5 Throughput Rate

The detector shall provide a positive *alarm indication* for the *test object* of the appropriate *object size class* and its orientation from which the "minimum detection conditions" were determined (see sec. 2.3.1) for the *test object* moving at a speed of 1 m/s ± 0.05 m/s at the z-axis positions of 86 cm ± 0.5 cm, 144 cm ± 0.5 cm, and 178 cm ± 0.5 cm when tested in accordance with section 3.2.7, and the results shall be recorded.

2.4 Operating Requirements

2.4.1 Operator Controls

Only those controls required to operate the equipment shall be accessible to the operator. Other controls and adjustments that affect the detector performance shall be inaccessible to the operator. The detector shall be self-testing upon turn-on without any adjustment required by the operator and shall be continuously self-testing during the period of operation with automatic self-adjusting, if required. The following operator controls shall be provided:

2.4.1.1 Power On/Off Switch

The detector shall have a power on/off switch.

2.4.1.2 Audio Alarm On/Off Switch

The detector shall have a means for selectively disabling the audio alarm.

2.4.1.3 Detector Reset Button

The detector shall reset automatically to the set program parameters in the event of a detector or system failure or overload. There shall be a detector reset button to reset the detector such that program parameters are not affected if the automatic reset for a detector overload condition is not functioning properly.

2.4.1.4 Detector Sensitivity Programming

If provided, the detector sensitivity shall be programmed electronically, and if the detector is designed for multiple *object size classes*, then it shall have settings that correspond to the appropriate *object size classes*.

2.4.2 Interference

2.4.2.1 Electromagnetic

2.4.2.1.1 Emission

The detector, when adjusted to meet the requirements of section 2.3.3, shall meet the requirements of EN 50081–1, as amended.

2.4.2.1.2 Susceptibility/Immunity

2.4.2.1.2.1 General Immunity Requirements

The detector, when adjusted to meet the requirements of section 2.3.3, shall not provide a *positive alarm indication* when tested in accordance with EN 50082–1, as amended.

2.4.2.1.2.2 Radiated Magnetic Field

The detector, when adjusted to meet the requirements of section 2.3.3, shall not provide a *positive alarm indication* when tested in accordance with MIL–STD–461E, Method RS101, as amended, to the limits for Navy applications.

2.4.2.2 Metallic Interference

2.4.2.2.1 Stationary Objects

The detector, when adjusted to meet the requirements of section 2.3.3 and tested in accordance with sections 3.4.1 and 3.4.2, shall not produce a *positive alarm indication* when no *test object* is presented to the detector.

2.4.2.2.2 Moving Objects, Moving Metal Door

The detector shall not produce a *positive alarm indication* when operated near a moving metal door, as tested in accordance with section 3.4.3, but shall produce a *positive alarm indication* for each appropriate *test object* and its orientation providing a minimum response as determined according to section 2.3.1 for the *test object* moving at a speed of 1.0 m/s ± 0.05 m/s at each *test measurement location* when operated while such a door is moving in accordance with section 3.4.3.

2.4.2.3 Body Interference

The detector, when adjusted to meet the requirements of section 2.3.3, shall not produce a *positive alarm indication* when tested in accordance with section 3.2.6; the results shall be recorded and a report provided.

2.4.2.4 Multiple Object Interference (*Large Object Size Class* Only)

The detector shall produce a *positive alarm indication* when tested in accordance with section 3.2.8; the results shall be recorded and a report provided.

2.4.3 Environmental Ranges and Conditions

The detector or all of its components and their interconnections shall meet the requirements of all of the following standards. The requirements of section 2.1 and section 2.5 shall not be affected by the tests described in this section. The requirements given in this section shall be applied appropriately for either indoor, sheltered outdoor, or outdoor detector models. The requirements of this section shall be exhibited by no less than the first production unit for each unique detector model and for any physical modifications to that model. The tests listed in section 2.4.3 shall be performed on the same unit. The detector, if tested for any of the tests listed in section 2.4.3, shall exhibit no observable changes in the detection performance specification given in section 2.3.3.

2.4.3.1 Temperature Stability and Range

2.4.3.1.1 Indoor, Sheltered Outdoor

The detector shall operate over the ambient temperature range of at least 0 °C to 46 °C (32 °F to 115 °F). The detector shall be tested in accordance with MIL–STD–810F Method 501.4, Procedure II, at 46 °C ± 3 °C after being exposed to that temperature continuously for 24 h ± 1 h. The detector then shall be cooled to 0 °C ± 3 °C within 4 h ± 0.5 h and tested in accordance with MIL–STD–810F Method 502.4, Procedure II, at 0 °C ± 3 °C after being exposed to that temperature continuously for 24 h ± 1 h.

2.4.3.1.2 Outdoor

The detector shall operate over the ambient temperature range of at least -37 °C to 65 °C (-35 °F to 149 °F). The detector shall be tested in accordance with MIL–STD–810F Method 501.4, Procedure II, at 65 °C ± 3 °C after being exposed to that temperature continuously for 24 h ± 1 h. The detector then shall be cooled to -37 °C ± 3 °C within 4 h ± 0.5 h and tested in accordance with MIL–STD–810F Method 502.4, Procedure II, at -37 °C ± 3 °C after being exposed to that temperature continuously for 24 h ± 1 h.

2.4.3.2 Relative Humidity Stability and Range

The detector shall be tested in accordance with the requirements of MIL–STD–810F Method 507.4, as amended.

2.4.3.3 Salt Fog, Sheltered Outdoor and Outdoor

The detector shall be tested in accordance with the requirements of MIL–STD–810F Method 509.4, as amended.

2.4.3.4 Environmental Protection

2.4.3.4.1 Indoor

The detector shall meet or exceed the requirements for compliance to IEC 60529 classification IP41.

2.4.3.4.2 Sheltered Outdoor

The detector shall meet or exceed the requirements for compliance to IEC 60529 classification IP53.

2.4.3.4.3 Outdoor

The detector shall meet or exceed the requirements for compliance to IEC 60529 classification IP55.

2.4.3.5 Solar Radiation (Sunshine), Outdoor Only

The detector shall be tested in accordance with and meet the requirements of MIL–STD–810F Method 505.4, Procedure 1, as amended.

2.5 Mechanical Specifications and Requirements

2.5.1 Dimensions and Weight

The detector shall be designed so the interior of the portal through which people will walk has the following dimensions:

a. Height, minimum: 195 cm (77 in).
b. Width, minimum: 71 cm (28 in) unless required to comply with that specified by the American Disabilities Act.
c. Depth, maximum: 91 cm (36 in).

The detector shall have a mass of less than 100 kg (220 lb).

2.5.2 Durability/Ruggedness

The detector or all of its components and their interconnections shall meet the requirements of the following standards. The requirements of section 2.1 and section 2.4 shall not be affected by the tests described in this section. The tests listed in section 2.5.2 shall be performed on the same unit.

2.5.2.1 Impact Resistance

The detector, if tested for any of the tests listed in section 2.5.2.1, shall exhibit no observable changes in the detection performance specification given in section 2.3.3.

2.5.2.1.1 Shock

The detector shall be tested in accordance with the requirements of IEC 68–2–27 1987, as amended, using the half-sine pulse shape with a nominal peak acceleration of 5 g (50 m/s^2) and nominal pulse duration of 30 ms.

2.5.2.1.2 Bump

The detector shall be disassembled and the control unit and columns of the detector shall be tested independently and in accordance with the requirements of IEC 68–2–29 1987, as amended, using 100 bumps each with a nominal peak acceleration of 10 g (100 m/s^2) and nominal pulse duration of 16 ms.

2.5.2.2 Pressure Resistance

The detector should be capable of being secured in place to prevent being tipped over or slipping as a result of casual bumping or pushing. The detector shall be capable of withstanding the forces described below.

2.5.2.2.1 Slide

A force shall be applied at 1.0 m ± 0.1 m (39 in ± 4 in) above the *ground surface* in the direction of passage until the detector starts to slide. The detector shall be capable of withstanding the force of 200 N (45 lb) without sliding.

2.5.2.2.2 Tip-Over

The detector shall be tested in accordance with section 5.4 of American Society for Testing and Materials (ASTM) Designation F 1468–95, as amended. The test results shall be recorded and a report provided. The detector shall be capable of withstanding a force of 600 N (135 lb) applied to the detector at 1.3 m ± 0.1 m (51 in ± 4 in) above the *ground surface* in the direction of passage without tipping.

2.6 Functional Requirements

2.6.1 Program Storage

The detector shall have a means of storing the program and detection sensitivity settings in the event of loss or disruption of ac power to maintain the calibration and setup of the walk-through metal detector parameters.

2.6.2 Alarm Indicators

2.6.2.1 Audible Alarm Indicators

All audible indicators (other than an earphone) shall produce an alarm-state sound pressure level 0.8 m ± 0.08 m from the detector of 85 dB_{SPL} ± 5 dB_{SPL} measured in accordance with section 3.3.2. For status indicators, the audible alarm shall be a two-state audible alarm: active (alarm state) and inactive (nonalarm state). The two-state alarm indicator shall produce no sound in the nonalarm state.

2.6.2.2 Earphone Jack, Optional

If an earphone jack is supplied with the walk-through metal detector, the earphone shall disable the audible *alarm indicator* when the earphone is plugged into the earphone jack.

2.6.2.3 Visual Alarm Indicators

Any visible *alarm indication* shall be readily perceptible when tested in accordance with section 3.3.3. The visual *alarm indicators* shall be a two-state visual alarm: active (illuminating) and inactive (nonilluminating).

2.6.2.4 Metal Object Detection

The detector shall have a two-state audible *alarm indicator* and a visual *alarm indicator* which shall alarm to indicate the presence of a *test object* in the portal region. The alarm state for the metal-object-detection visual *alarm indicator* shall be active (illuminating), and the nonalarm state shall be inactive (nonilluminating). The metal-object-detection visual *alarm indicator* shall be distinct from any other visual *alarm indicators*.

2.6.2.5 AC Power Out-of-Range Condition

The detector shall have a two-state audible *alarm indicator* to indicate the ac power level is out of specification and shall be activated if the state of the ac power changes to a level that can cause an observable change in detection performance specifications.

2.6.2.6 System Status

The detector shall have a two-state audible *alarm indicator* or a visual *alarm indicator* to indicate the operational state of the detector system and shall be activated if the operational state of the detector can cause a degradation of the detection performance required by this standard. The system status visual *alarm indicator* shall be inactive (nonilluminating) if the system status is acceptable and shall be active (illuminating) if a system status problem exists. The system status visual *alarm indicator* shall be distinct from any other visual *alarm indicators*.

2.6.2.7 Detection Ready State Violation

The detector shall have a two-state audible *alarm indicator* or a visual *alarm indicator* to indicate passage of a person through the detector when it was not in the ready state as described in section 2.6.2.8 and shall be activated if a person attempts to pass through the detector when it is not in the ready state. The visual *alarm indicator* shall be active (illuminating) if a person attempts to pass through the detector when it is not in the ready state, and inactive (nonilluminating) otherwise.

2.6.2.8 Detection Ready State (Stop/Go)

The detector shall have clearly visible to the approaching traffic, a visual indicator showing the ready state of the detector; that is, whether the detector is ready to allow a pass through or not. The ready state shall be indicated by a green and red visual indicator; the green visual indicator shall denote readiness, and the red visual indicator shall denote lack of readiness. The green light (or "Go" light) shall indicate that the detector is ready for a person to enter and pass through the detector, and the red light (or "Stop" light) shall indicate that the detector is not ready for a person to enter the detector.

2.6.3 Detection Signal Output Connector

The detector shall have an electrical connector from which either an analog or digital output signal is obtained. This signal represents the magnitude of the detector's response to an object and is the detector signal upon which an *alarm indication* is based. If the output signal is analog, the connector shall be coaxial where the inner conductor provides the signal path and the outer conductor of the connector provides signal ground or return. For detectors consisting of more than one generator and/or sensor, such as in multizone detectors, there shall be a *detection signal output connector* for each sensor or sensor circuit unless the sensor or sensor circuit outputs are multiplexed together. If the sensor circuits of a multizone system are multiplexed, the *detection signal output connector* can be used to monitor the output of each sensor or sensor circuit.

2.6.4 Interchangeability

Any model detector manufactured by the same manufacturer shall be compatible with previous revisions of the same model (backwardly compatible). In particular, the following components shall be backwardly compatible:

a. Replacement parts.
b. Error codes.
c. Program codes.
d. Diagnostic warnings.
e. Connectors.

2.6.5 Field Servicing

The detector shall be designed for ease of maintenance; that is, to clean, inspect, adjust, align, and repair. The electronics shall be of modular design and easily accessible for maintenance and repair.

2.7 Detector Mount

The manufacturer shall provide with each detector, if requested, a *detector mount* for positioning the walk-through metal detector for performance tests. See figure 2. The *detector mount* (see fig. 5) shall comply with the requirements of section 2.1.2 and shall meet the following specifications:

a. Relative permeability = 1.0 ± 0.001.
b. Electrical conductivity < 10^{-8} Siemens/m.
c. Mass ≤ 50 kg (110 lb).

d. Flatness of surface mating to *reference surface* ± 0.5 mm (0.041 in).
e. Hold the detector in position.
f. Mate with the *reference surface* (see fig. 6).
g. Fastener holes that align with each of the (two to four) 3/8-16 fastener holes of the *reference surface* (see fig. 6).
h. Hold the detector so that the *detector plane* and the x-z plane of the *measurement coordinate system* are parallel to within ± 1 degree.
i. Hold the detector so that the *detector plane* is 0.5 m ± 0.01 m from the *reference surface* (see figs. 2 and 6).
j. Position the *detector floor* at a height of 32.5 cm ± 0.5 cm above the *ground surface* (see fig. 5).
k. Provide a 1 cm ± 0.1 cm groove for the steel reinforced floor test panel at a height of 22.5 cm ± 0.5 cm above the *ground surface* (see fig. 5).

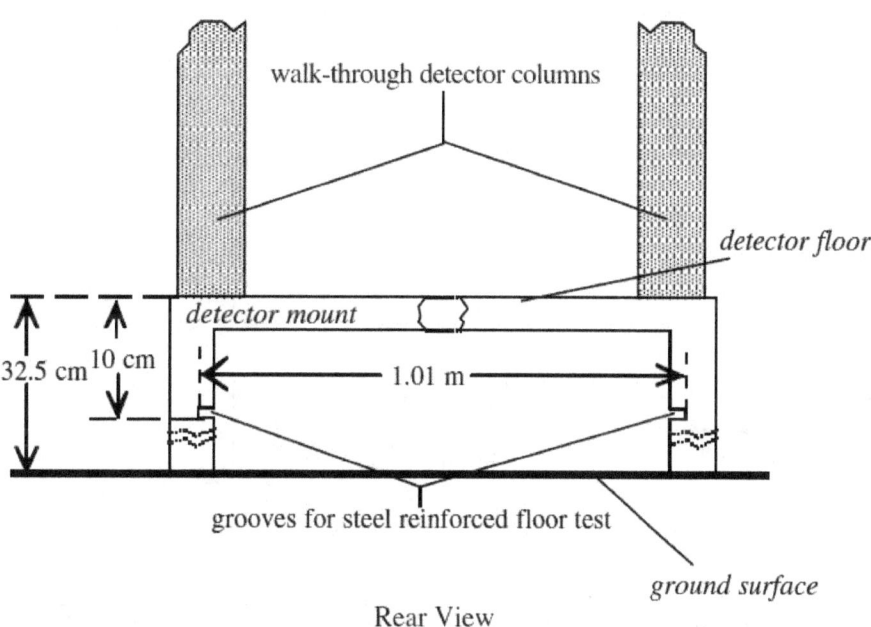

Figure 5. Drawing of the detector mount showing the positioning of grooves for the steel reinforced floor test

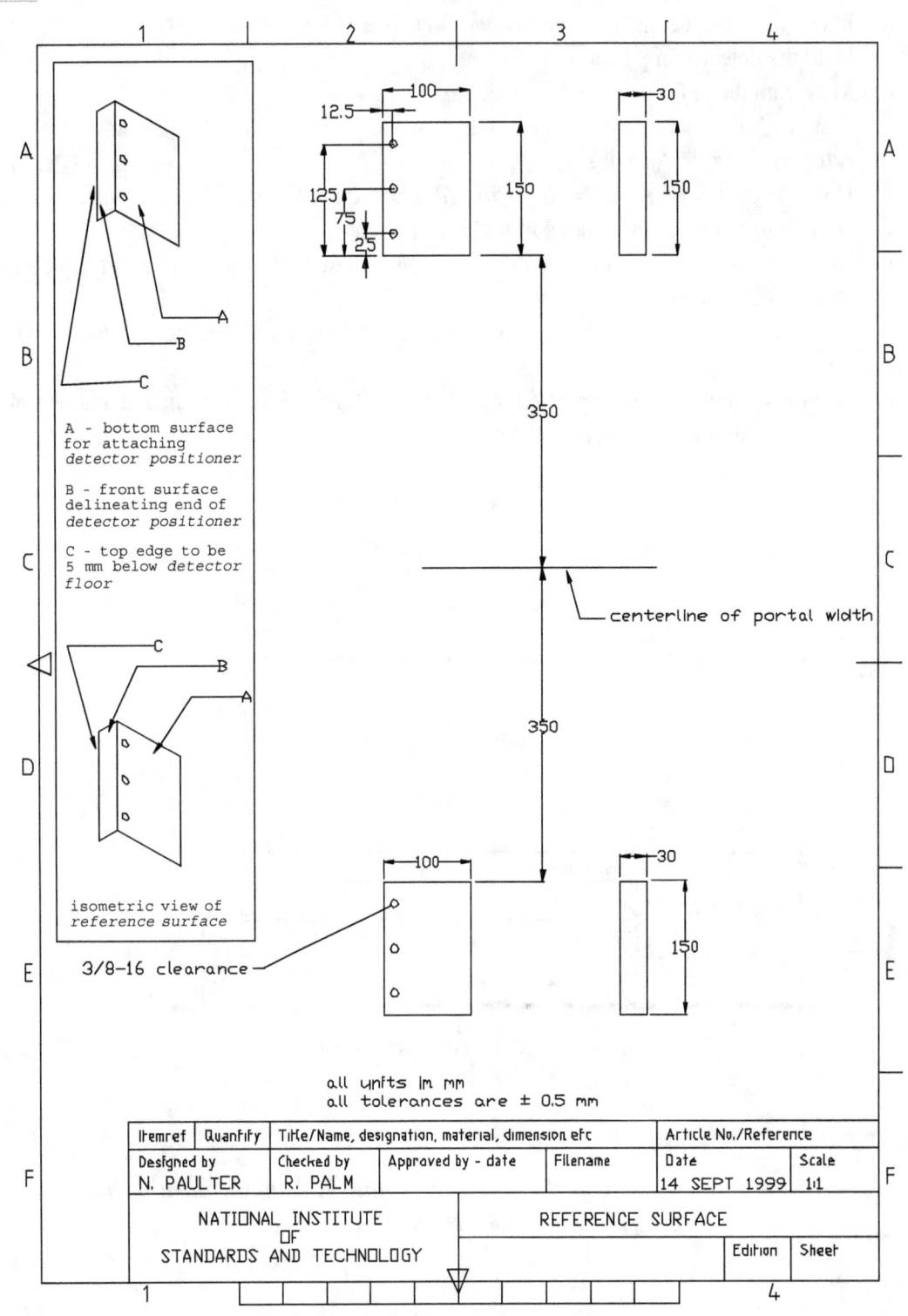

Figure 6. Mechanical drawing of the reference surface

2.8 Quality Control and Assurance

2.8.1 Quality System

The manufacturer shall meet the requirements of ISO 9001:2000, as amended.

2.8.2 Testing and Calibration Laboratories

Laboratories performing testing and calibration of the detector and/or its components shall meet the requirements of IEC 17025.

2.8.3 Measurement Equipment and Processes

All measurement equipment and processes shall meet the requirements of ISO 10012–1 and ISO 10012–2.

2.8.4 Burn-In

Power-on dynamic burn-in testing for a set of metal detectors of the same model is required in accordance with section 3.5. The set shall consist of m detectors of the same type and model selected using simple random sampling methods and tested without replacement (where $m = \text{ceil}\left(\dfrac{0.1 M k_M}{0.1 k_M + 0.01 M}\right)$, M is the number of the manufactured detectors of the same model, ceil is a function that returns the smallest integer greater than or equal to its argument, and k_M is the coverage factor for the 99 % confidence interval, see Table B.1 of B.N. Taylor and C.E. Kuyatt, NIST Technical Note 1297, *Guidelines for Evaluating and Expressing the Uncertainty of NIST Measurement Results*, U.S. Government Printing Office, Washington, DC, 1994). The manufacturer shall provide the test results of this randomly selected set of same type and model detectors.

2.9 Documentation

The manufacturer shall provide the following list of deliverable items with each detector unless otherwise indicated.

2.9.1 Operating Instructions

The manufacturer or distributor shall supply with each detector an operator's manual that shall contain at least the following information:

a. The purpose of the detector.
b. A description of operator controls.

c. A listing of the operating features.
d. A description of the detection principles and detector capabilities.
e. A block diagram showing the major internal functional components.
f. An exposure warning that states "This Device May Affect Personal Medical Electronic Devices." This warning shall be in place until such time that the Food and Drug Administration or some other competent Federal agency requires a different warning or has determined that no such warning is necessary.

2.9.2 Operator Training Instructions and Videotape or CD-ROM

A training package shall be supplied upon request that will provide operators with the information necessary to acquire the technical and operational skills required to conduct effective screening with the detector. The training package shall include an audio/visual videotape or CD-ROM as well as an operator's manual. For additional guidance in formulating the operator training package, review *A Users' Guide for Hand-Held and Walk-Through Metal Weapon Detectors*, published by the National Institute of Justice. The manufacturer shall have demonstrated the effectiveness of the training material when 50 % of the test group receiving the training understands the operation of the detector, passes a written test, and operates the detector successfully. The test group shall consist of at least 10 people with only a high school education.

2.9.3 Technical Manual

A technical manual shall be provided upon request which contains all of the information that could be required by a technician to troubleshoot, maintain, and repair the equipment to the component level.

2.9.4 Technical Training Manual and Videotape or CD-ROM

A self-study training package shall be provided upon request for use by site maintenance technicians. The training package must consist of an audio/visual videotape or CD-ROM as well as a technical manual that provides detailed explanations of circuit theory and maintenance procedures.

2.9.5 Technical Specifications

The manufacturer shall provide, upon request, a detailed listing of all relevant specifications of the detector. This listing shall include at a minimum:

a. Detector *object size class* (as defined in sec. 1.2.14).
b. Mechanical drawings of the detector with dimensions in metric units.
c. Mass of the detector.
d. Allowable range of ac line power supply voltage.
e. Battery type, quantity, and life.
f. Maximum magnetic field strength that can be found on the detector surface.

g. If applicable, operating frequency and, if applicable, modulation parameters.
h. If applicable, pulse repetition rate, pulse duration, and pulse transition duration.
i. Operating ambient temperature range.

2.9.6 Certifications of Test, Inspection, and Conformance

The manufacturer shall provide upon request a certification of all mandatory tests, test procedures, testing laboratories, compliance to required standards, a record of the test results for the detector, and the identities of all the companies, laboratories, and/or organizations conducting the tests.

2.9.7 Suggested Maintenance Schedule

The manufacturer shall provide a preventive maintenance schedule and a detailed list of the technical skills, computer hardware, and software tools required.

2.9.8 Installation Instructions

The manufacturer shall provide detailed instructions for the location and installation of the walk-through metal detector. The manufacturer shall also provide instructions for battery installation and specify the type and quantity of batteries required.

3. PERFORMANCE TESTING PROCEDURES

The detector shall meet the detection performance requirements for each *object size class* in which it is required to operate. The detection performance shall be evaluated by the test methods described in this section. The manufacturer shall record and provide the test results on the report forms mentioned in section 6 of this randomly selected set of same type and model detectors.

3.1 General Test Conditions

3.1.1 Test Location

The distance between any metal object other than a *test object* shall be at least 15 cm from the *detector floor*, at least 15 cm from the topmost part of the detector, and at least 0.8 cm from any side or outward projections of any side of the detector.

3.1.2 Environment

At the time of the tests, the ambient temperature shall be in the range specified in section 2.4.3.1 for the appropriate application (indoor, sheltered outdoor, or outdoor); the relative humidity shall be noncondensing.

3.1.3 Preparations

The walk-through metal detector shall be installed according to the manufacturer's instructions. Any setup or calibration adjustments specified in the operator's manual shall be performed if required.

3.2 Detection Performance Tests

For walk-through metal detectors that contain more than one generator and/or sensor, the *detector response* shall be recorded for each generator or sensor appropriate for the location of the *test object* within the portal region of the detector.

3.2.1 Object Size Classes

If the detector can be adjusted to provide an *alarm indication* for both *large object size* and *medium object size*, the detection performance test shall be performed for each *object size class*. The detection performance shall be evaluated by the test methods described in this section.

3.2.2 Equipment

3.2.2.1 Test Objects

Test objects shall be as described in section 5. There are up to three orientation holes on up to three surfaces of the *test object* (encased replica of a threat item). The tapped hole on each surface of the *test objects* is labeled with an "A" (see mechanical drawings in sec. 5 showing the encased *test object*) and is the center of rotation of the different orientations. The *test objects* shall be oriented such that their orienting holes that are being used are facing the *three-axis positioning system* and the hole labeled "A" is below the other orientation hole being used. Labeling for the *test object* orientation shall use two characters: the first character indicates in which quadrant of the mechanical drawing the specified orientation can be found, and the second character indicates the position of the unused hole relative to the hole labeled "A." The quadrant designations are given as follows:

- "1" indicates bottom left.
- "2" indicate bottom right.
- "3" indicates top left.
- "4" indicates top right.

Not all quadrants are used. For the second character, "L" indicates that the unused hole is to the left of the hole labeled "A," and "R" indicates that the unused hole is to the right of the hole labeled "A."

3.2.2.2 Three-Axes Positioning System

The *three-axes positioning system* shall meet the following requirements:

a. Displacement, x and y axes: ≥1 m.
b. Displacement, z axis: ≥ 2 m.
c. Position accuracy, each axis: 1 mm.
d. Position repeatability, each axis: 1 mm.
e. Maximum slew speed, y axis: ≥ 2 m/s.

3.2.2.3 Magnetic Field Sensor

The magnetic field sensor shall have a frequency response bandwidth at least five times greater than the bandwidth of the generated magnetic field, provide a rms voltage output, and have dimensions less than or equal to 4 cm x 4 cm x 4 cm.

3.2.2.4 Voltmeter

The ac voltmeter shall have a bandwidth at least five times greater than the bandwidth of the generated magnetic field, allow computer control and data retrieval, and have a variable gain input with at least 10-bit resolution full scale.

3.2.2.5 Microphone (Audible *Alarm Indicators*)

The microphone is the audible *alarm indication* detector. It shall be used to detect an audible *positive alarm indication*, be capable of detecting the audible *alarm indication* as described in section 2.6.2, and provide an analog output that can be interfaced to the computer controller (see sec. 3.2.2.8).

3.2.2.6 Light Detector (Visible *Alarm Indicators*)

The light detector is the visible *alarm indication* detector. It shall be used to detect a visible *positive alarm indication*, be capable of being attached directly to the visual alarm indicator, and provide an analog electrical output that can be interfaced to the computer controller (see sec. 3.2.2.8).

3.2.2.7 Detector Positioner

The *detector positioner* is a nonconductive, nonmagnetic device that provides a *reference surface* on which to securely attach the *detector mount* and that maintains the *detector plane* at a fixed location in the *measurement coordinate system* relative to the *three-axes positioning system*. A detailed mechanical drawing of the *reference surface* is provided in figure 6.

3.2.2.8 Computer Controller

The computer controller shall have installed and operational all necessary hardware and software for providing instrument control and data acquisition.

3.2.3 Detection Sensitivity

3.2.3.1 Initial Procedures

Ensure that the voltmeter, *alarm indication* detector, and *three-axes positioning system* are connected to the computer controller and that the detection signal output connector (see sec. 2.6.3) is connected to the voltmeter (for analog signals) or to the computer (for digital signals). Turn on the voltmeter, *alarm indication* detector, computer controller, and positioning system and verify proper operation of the measurement system. Ensure that the walk-through metal detector is securely located and positioned in the *measurement coordinate system*. Attach the *test object* with the proper orientation to the positioning system. Turn on the walk-through metal detector and ensure that its output functions properly by noting a change in the magnitude of the detection signal and activation of the *alarm indication* as a metal object is brought near the detector. Ensure that the *test object* does not hit any objects while in motion.

3.2.3.2 Performing the Measurement

The scan limits for the x-axis scan shall be the boundaries of the *test measurement grid locations*. The center for both the x and z direction scans shall be the *detector axis* (see fig. 1). Set the computer program to perform a one-meter-long y-axis scan at the specified speed that is perpendicular to, passes through, and is centered at the *detector plane*. Set the x-axis and z-axis positions to the most negative scan limits. Perform a y-axis scan, measure the signal present at the detection signal output connector (see sec. 2.6.3), and record this measurement as the y-axis is scanned in the forward direction. (Alternatively, perform a y-axis scan and record any *positive alarm indication* in the forward direction using the *alarm indication* detector.) Move the x axis in 5 cm ± 0.1 cm increments and repeat the y-axis scan measurement for each x-axis increment until the x-axis positive scan limit is reached. Move the z axis in 5 cm ± 0.1 cm increments while repeating the x-axis incremented motion and the y-axis scan measurement until the z-axis positive scan limit is reached. (Alternatively, adjust the detector sensitivity settings either after each scan has been performed or after scans at all of the *test measurement grid locations* have been performed and determine the threshold for *test object* detection at each *test measurement grid location*.) Record the average detection signal value for each y-axis scan and report these values. Record any *positive alarm indication* using the *alarm indication* detector as the y-axis scan is being performed. (Alternatively, record the detector threshold sensitivity settings for each y-axis scan and report these values.)

3.2.4 Speed

3.2.4.1 Initial Procedures

Ensure that the *alarm indication* detector and *three-axes positioning system* are connected to the computer controller. Turn on the *alarm indication* detector, the computer controller, and the *three-axes positioning system* and verify proper operation of the measurement system. Ensure that the walk-through metal detector is securely located and positioned within the *measurement coordinate system*. Adjust the detector to the appropriate sensitivity setting. Attach the *test object* with the proper orientation to the *three-axes positioning system*. Turn on the walk-through metal detector and ensure that its output functions properly by noting a change in the *alarm indication* detector reading as a metal object is brought near the portal region. Ensure that the *test object* does not hit any objects while in motion.

3.2.4.2 Performing the Measurement

Set the computer program to perform a one-meter-long y-axis scan at the specified speed that is perpendicular to, passes through, and is centered at the *detector plane* at the specified x-axis and z-axis position. Record any *positive alarm indication* using the *alarm indication* detector as the y-axis scan is being performed.

3.2.5 Discrimination

3.2.5.1 Initial Procedures

See section 3.2.4.1.

3.2.5.2 Performing the Measurement

Set the computer program to perform a one-meter-long y-axis scan that is perpendicular to, passes through, and is centered at the *detector plane* at the x-axis position of 0 cm ± 0.5 cm centered on the z-axis and z-axis position of 60 cm ± 0.5 cm. Attach the three-axis positioning system to the *innocuous item test object* holder (see sec. 5.4.3) at the designated location on the *innocuous item test object* holder. Perform the y-axis scan and record any *positive alarm indication* using the *alarm indication* detector as the y-axis scan is being performed.

3.2.6 Body Interference

The detector shall be placed in a sufficiently stable location so that walking through the portal does not cause a positive *alarm indication*.

3.2.6.1 Initial Procedures

Select a *clean tester*. Ensure that the *alarm indication* detector is connected to the computer. Turn on the *alarm indication* detector and computer controller and verify proper operation of the measurement system. Ensure that the detector sensitivity settings are appropriate for the desired *object size class*.

3.2.6.2 Performing the Measurement

Direct the *clean tester* to walk through the center of the portal of the metal detector at a speed of approximately 1.0 m/s. Record any *positive alarm indication* using the *alarm indication* detector as the *clean tester* passes through the portal.

3.2.7 Throughput Rate

3.2.7.1 Initial Procedures

See section 3.2.4.1. Position the *test object* support platform (see sec. 3.2.7.3) so that the *detector axis* is parallel to and the *detector plane* perpendicular to the top surface of the support platform and the z-axis of the detector is centered ± 1 cm in both the width and the length of the support platform. A forward-going scan direction moves the *test object* farther away from the three-axis positioning system and through the detector portal. A backward-going scan direction moves the *test object* through the detector portal and closer to the three-axis positioning system. The delay is the difference between the stopping time of the forward-going scan and the starting time of the negative-going scan. This procedure requires two *test objects*. The first *test object* is attached to the positioning system and is the one referenced in section 2.3.5. The second *test object*, a *large size test object*, is not attached to the positioning system and is pushed by the first *test object* through the detector portal during the forward-going scan.

3.2.7.2 Performing the Measurement

Set the computer program to perform a one-meter-long y-axis scan at the specified measurement conditions and set the y-axis scan position to -0.5 m ± 1 cm from the *detector plane*. Rest the top panel of the *test object* support platform (see sec. 3.2.7.3) on the dowel pins closest to the specified z-axis position. Attach the first *test object* to the positioning system. Place the second *test object* on top of the *test object* support platform, against the first *test object*, and orient the second *test object* as shown in the bottom right of the mechanical drawing of the encased replica (see sec. 5.1). Perform the forward-going y-axis scan, record any *positive alarm indication* using the *alarm indication* detector as the forward-going y-axis scan is being performed, record the time at which the forward-going y-axis scan terminated, wait for a delay of 2.0 s ± 0.05 s, perform the backward-going y-axis scan, and record any *positive alarm indication* using the *alarm indication* detector as the backward-going y-axis scan is being performed. Decrease the delay by 0.1 s ± 0.01 s, repeat the procedure described in the previous sentence until no *alarm indication* is observed for the backward-going y-axis scan, and record this delay for the specified z-axis position. Repeat this process for all specified z-axis positions. Take the longest of this set of recorded delays, add 0.1 s to get the corrected delay, and divide 60 s/min by the corrected delay to get the throughput rate.

3.2.7.3 Test-Object Support Platform

This section contains a description of a *test object* support platform. The purpose of the support platform is to provide a rest for the *test objects* at the *test measurement location* (see fig. 4) heights of 78 cm, 130 cm, and 178 cm. The test-object support platform shall be constructed using the following items and as shown in figures 7 and 8.

A. Cross pieces, 6 each, wood "1x4," 65 cm ± 1 cm long, with the following hole pattern:
  Two holes each end
    9.5 mm ± 0.5 mm dia, through hole
    4 cm ± 0.1 cm from the end
    First hole 3 cm ± 0.1 cm from the top edge
    Second hole 6 cm ± 0.1 cm from the top edge
B. Sides, 2 each, plywood "1/2-inch," 101 cm ± 1 cm x 1.2 m ± 1 cm, with the following hole pattern:
  Three holes each along each short (101 cm) edge
    9.5 mm ± 0.5 mm dia, through hole
    2 cm ± 0.1 cm from the edge
    First hole 4.5 cm ± 0.1 cm from the bottom edge
    Second hole 62.5 cm ± 0.1 cm from the bottom edge
    Third hole 96.5 cm ± 0.1 cm from the bottom edge
C. Posts, 4 each, wood "2x4," 1.8 m ± 1 cm long, with the following hole pattern:
  Three holes each centered on the narrow side of the "2x4," for side (item B) attachment
    9.5 mm ± 0.5 mm dia, 2 cm ± 0.5 cm deep
    First hole 77.5 cm ± 0.1 cm from the bottom end
    Second hole 135.5 cm ± 0.1 cm from the bottom end
    Third hole 169.5 cm ± 0.1 cm from the bottom end
  Six holes each centered on the broad side of the "2x4," for cross piece (item A) attachment
    9.5 mm ± 0.5 mm dia, through holes
    First hole 76 cm ± 0.1 cm from the bottom end
    Second hole 79 cm ± 0.1 cm from the bottom end
    Third hole 134 cm ± 0.1 cm from the bottom end
    Fourth hole 137 cm ± 0.1 cm from the bottom end
    Fifth hole 168 cm ± 0.1 cm from the bottom end
    Sixth hole 171 cm ± 0.1 cm from the bottom end

D. Platform, 1 each, plywood "1/2-inch," 165 cm ± 1 cm x 44 cm ± 1 cm, with the following hole pattern:
   Three holes each on one narrow (44 cm) end:
      9.5 mm ± 0.5 mm dia, through holes
      2 cm ± 0.1 cm from the edge
      First hole 11 cm ± 0.1 cm from the bottom edge
      Second hole 22 cm ± 0.1 cm from the bottom edge
      Third hole 33 cm ± 0.1 cm from the bottom edge
E. Backstop, 1 each, wood "2x4," 44 cm ± 1 cm long, with the following hole pattern:
   Three holes each on one narrow side of the "2x4":
      9.5 mm ± 0.5 mm dia, 2 cm ± 0.5 cm deep
      2 cm ± 0.1 cm from the edge
      First hole 11 cm ± 0.1 cm from the bottom edge
      Second hole 22 cm ± 0.1 cm from the bottom edge
      Third hole 33 cm ± 0.1 cm from the bottom edge
F. Dowels, 39 each, hardwood, 9.5 mm ± 0.5 mm dia, 3 cm ± 0.5 cm long

Assemble item E to D using dowels (item F). Assemble item B to C and then A to C using dowels (item F).

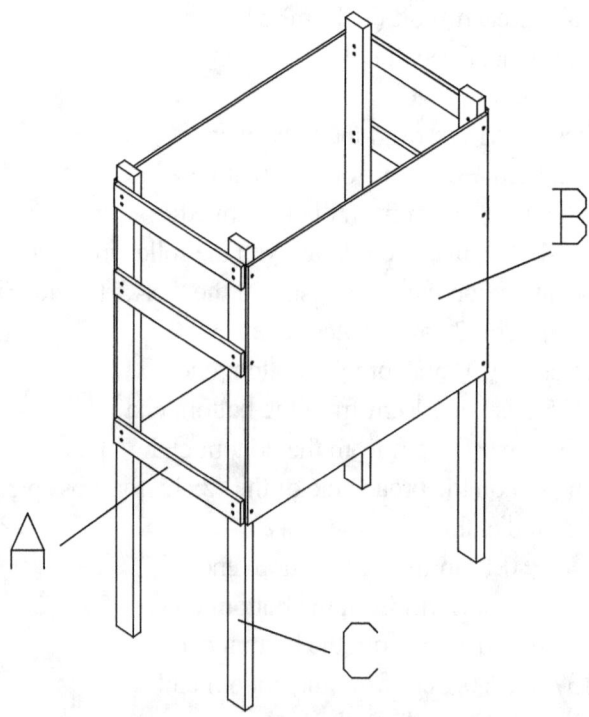

Figure 7. Drawing of assembly of items A, B, and C of test-object support platform

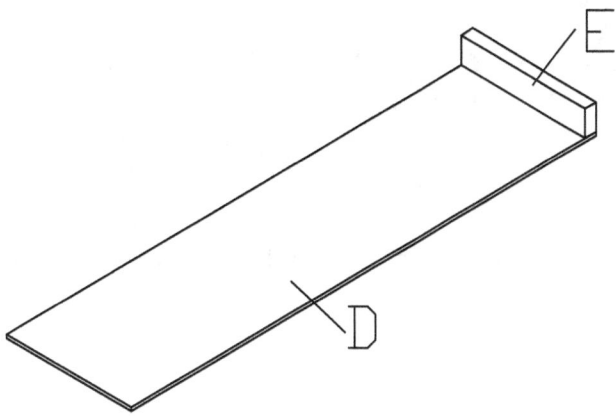

Figure 8. Drawing of assembly of items D and E of test-object support platform

3.2.8 Multiple Object Interference

3.2.8.1 Initial Procedures

See section 3.2.4.1. Attach the steel handgun replica (see mechanical drawing of the encased test object in sec. 5.1) to three-axis positioning system in the orientation shown in the bottom right of the drawing such that the plane through the point labeled "A" that is parallel to the bottom surface of the encasement is parallel to the *detector floor*. Attach the aluminum handgun replica, using the same orientation as that of the steel handgun replica, to the steel handgun replica using nonelectrically conductive nonmagnetic tape.

3.2.8.2 Performing the Measurement

Set the computer program to perform a one-meter-long y-axis scan at 1.0 m/s ± 0.1 m/s that is perpendicular to, passes through, and is centered at the *detector plane* at the x-axis position of 0 cm ± 1 cm centered on the z-axis at the z-axis position of 80 cm ± 1 cm. Perform the y-axis scan and record any *positive alarm indication* using the *alarm indication* detector as the y-axis scan is being performed. Repeat the y-axis scan for the z-axis position of 110 cm ± 1 cm and 130 cm ± 1 cm, and record any *positive alarm indication* using the *alarm indication* detector as the y-axis scan is being performed.

3.3 Alarm Indication Test

3.3.1 Equipment

3.3.1.1 Sound Level Meter

The sound pressure level meter shall comply with ANSI S1.4, 1971, for type 3, A-weighting, reference pressure 20 µPa.

3.3.1.2 Illumination Meter

The illumination meter shall be capable of measuring light levels of 25 lm/m^2 and 10,000 lm/m^2 with an error of not more than 10 %. The integrated spectral response shall be within 10 % of the Commission Internationale de l'Eclairage (CIE, the International Commission on Illumination) photopic curve.

3.3.2 Sound Pressure Level Test

Perform the test in an anechoic chamber or at an outdoor location, at least 6 m (20 ft) from any large object, where the ambient sound pressure level at the time of the test is not more than 53 dB$_{SPL}$. Position the sound pressure level meter microphone 0.80 m (31 in) from the detector. Measure the sound pressure level with the detector power applied and the *alarm indicator* in the nonalarm state. Then position the appropriate test object at a *test separation distance* of 5 cm (2 in) to produce an alarm, and again measure the sound pressure level.

3.3.3 Visible Alarm Indicator Test

Position the detector with its alarm indicator 0.80 m ± 0.05 m from the eyes, at a test site where the ambient illumination is 10 000 lm/m^2 ± 1000 lm/m^2. After waiting at least 3 min to allow for eye accommodation, turn on the detector and move a metal object near the detector to cause an alarm. Observe the indication. Repeat the test at a test site where the ambient illumination is 25 lux ± 2.5 lux.

3.4 Test for Operation Near a Metal Wall, Steel Reinforced Floor, or Moving Metal Door

3.4.1 Stationary Metal Objects, Wall

The effects of the proximity of a metal wall or floor on the performance of the walk-through metal detector is assessed using a metal test panel.

3.4.1.1 Metal Test Panel

The metal test panel shall be cold-finished sheet carbon steel AISI C1015 to C1020 with dimensions of 1 m ± 0.1 m by 1 m ± 0.1 m by 0.75 mm ± 0.13 mm and mounted in a nonelectrically conductive, nonmagnetizable frame to prevent bowing and bending of the metal test panel.

3.4.1.2 Test Procedure

Position the metal test panel such that its large surfaces are perpendicular to the *detector plane*, the x axis of the *measurement coordinate system* passes through the center of the metal test panel, and the x-axis separation between the metal test panel and the *detector axis* is 0.5 m ± 0.01 m. Note and record any *positive alarm indication* after the panel is positioned and test the metal detector according to section 2.3.3 without moving the metal test panel. Perform this test on both sides of the walk-through metal detector portal.

3.4.2 Steel Reinforced Floor

The effects of the proximity of a steel reinforced floor on the performance of the walk-through metal detector is assessed using a metal test panel.

3.4.2.1 Metal Test Panel, Steel Reinforced Floor

The test floor shall be cold-finished sheet carbon steel AISI C1015 to C1020 with dimensions of 1 m ± 0.01 m by 1 m ± 0.01 m by 2 mm ± 0.2 mm.

3.4.2.2 Test Procedure

Position the metal test panel such that it fits firmly in the grooves of the *detector mount* and is parallel with the *ground surface* (see fig. 5). Note and record any *positive alarm indication* after the panel is positioned and test the metal detector according to section 2.3.3 without moving the metal test panel.

3.4.3 Moving Metal Door

The effects of the proximity of a moving metal door on the performance of the walk-through metal detector is simulated using a pivoting metal test panel.

3.4.3.1 Metal Test Door

The metal test door shall consist of a metal plate made of cold-finished sheet carbon steel AISI C1015 to C1020 with dimensions of 2 m ± 0.02 m by 1 m ± 0.02 m by 2 mm ± 0.2 mm attached with hinges to a stationary wooden frame such that the metal plate can swing 180° without obstruction.

3.4.3.2 Test Procedure

Position the metal test door such that the plane defined by the position of the metal plate at 0° and 180° is parallel to the *detector plane*, the *detector axis* is in the plane of the metal plate when the metal plate is in the 90° position, and the edge of the metal plate closest to the detector is 2 m ± 0.1 m from *detector plane* when the metal plate is at the 90° position. Place the metal plate at the 0° position. Rotate the metal plate to the 180° position in 4 s ± 1 s and record any *positive alarm indications*.

3.5 Burn-In Test

The burn-in test is to be performed for a minimum of 160 consecutive hours, with the last 40 h failure free.

3.5.1 Cycling of the Equipment

Once each working shift (8 h), the detector shall be cycled on and off 10 times within 20 s and immediately (within 60 s) tested in accordance with section 2.3.3.

3.5.2 Performance Evaluation

Once each working shift (8 h), the detector shall be tested according to section 2.3.3 and section 2.3.4.

4. FIELD TESTING PROCEDURES

4.1 Large Object Size

The detector shall be turned on, and a *clean tester* shall walk through the detector portal carrying each of the *large object size test objects* described in section 5.1, one at a time, to assure that the objects are properly detected. The *clean tester* shall then walk through the detector portal carrying each of the appropriate *innocuous item test objects* described in section 5.4.1 to assure that the objects are not detected. Repeat this test three times at pass-through speeds ranging from approximately 0.5 m/s to approximately 1.5 m/s to assure proper detector performance.

4.2 Medium Object Size

The detector shall be turned on and a *clean tester* shall walk through the detector portal carrying each of the *medium object size test objects* described in section 5.2, one at a time, to assure that the objects are properly detected. The *clean tester* shall then walk through the detector portal carrying each of the appropriate *innocuous item test objects* described in section 5.4.2 to assure that the objects are not detected. Repeat this test three times at pass-through speeds ranging from approximately 0.5 m/s to approximately 1.5 m/s to assure proper detector performance.

4.3 Small Object Size

The detector shall be turned on and a *clean tester* shall walk through the detector portal carrying each of the *small object size test objects* described in section 5.3, one at a time, to assure that the objects are properly detected. Repeat this test three times at pass-through speeds ranging from approximately 0.5 m/s to approximately 1.5 m/s to assure proper detector performance.

5. TEST OBJECTS DESCRIPTION

This section contains mechanical drawings of the *test objects*. The *test objects* are encased replicas of threat items. The dimensions in all the mechanical drawings of this section are in units of millimeters (mm).

5.1 Large Object Size Test Objects

The following mechanical drawings are of the replica of the *large object size* item that is considered a threat to an officer, a prisoner, an inmate, and the public safety. The *large object size* threat item is a handgun. The mechanical drawings are arranged in the following order: the mechanical drawing of the replica of the handgun and the location of the replica within the encasement. Three replicas are made and encased, one from each of the materials indicated in the drawings.

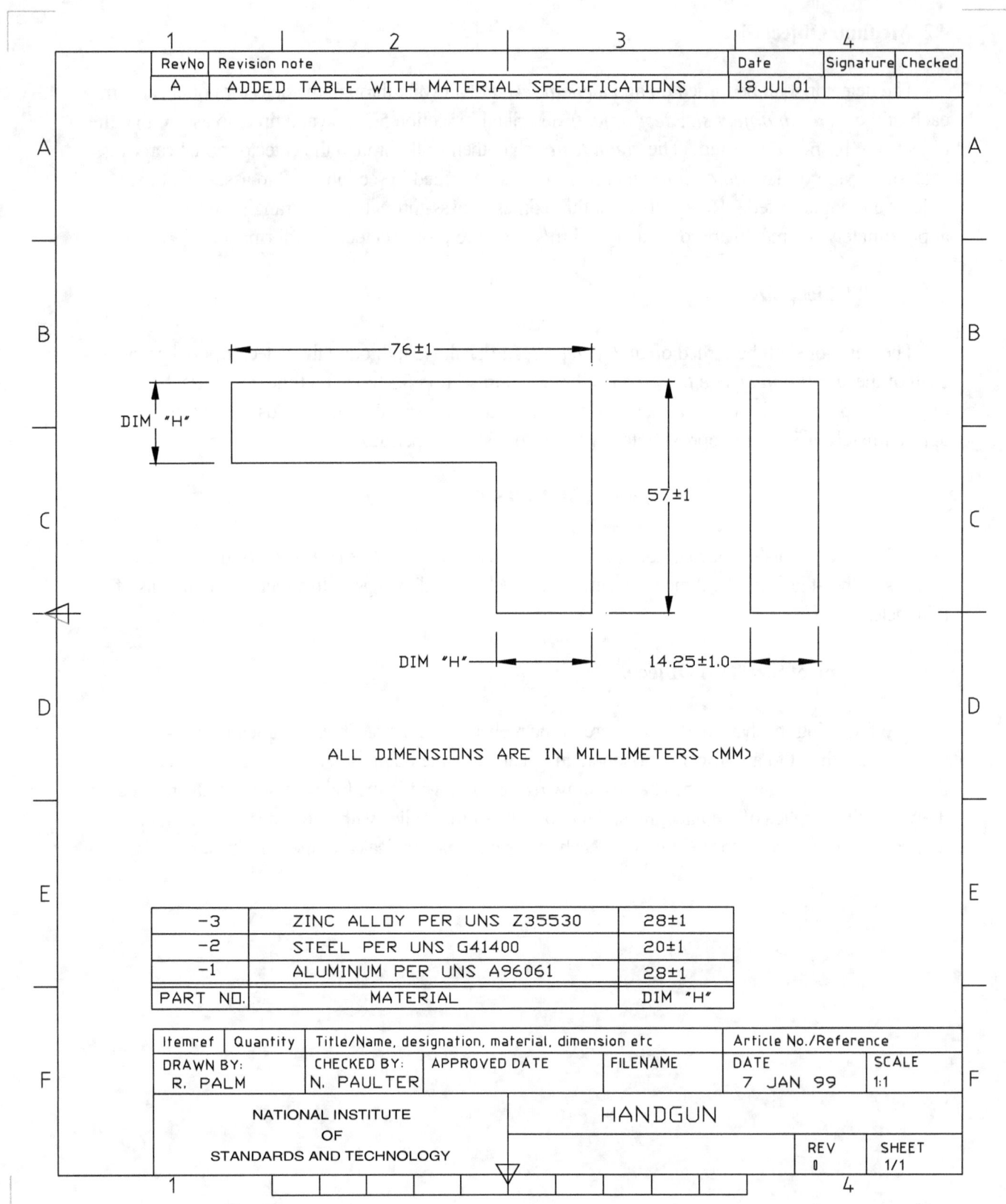

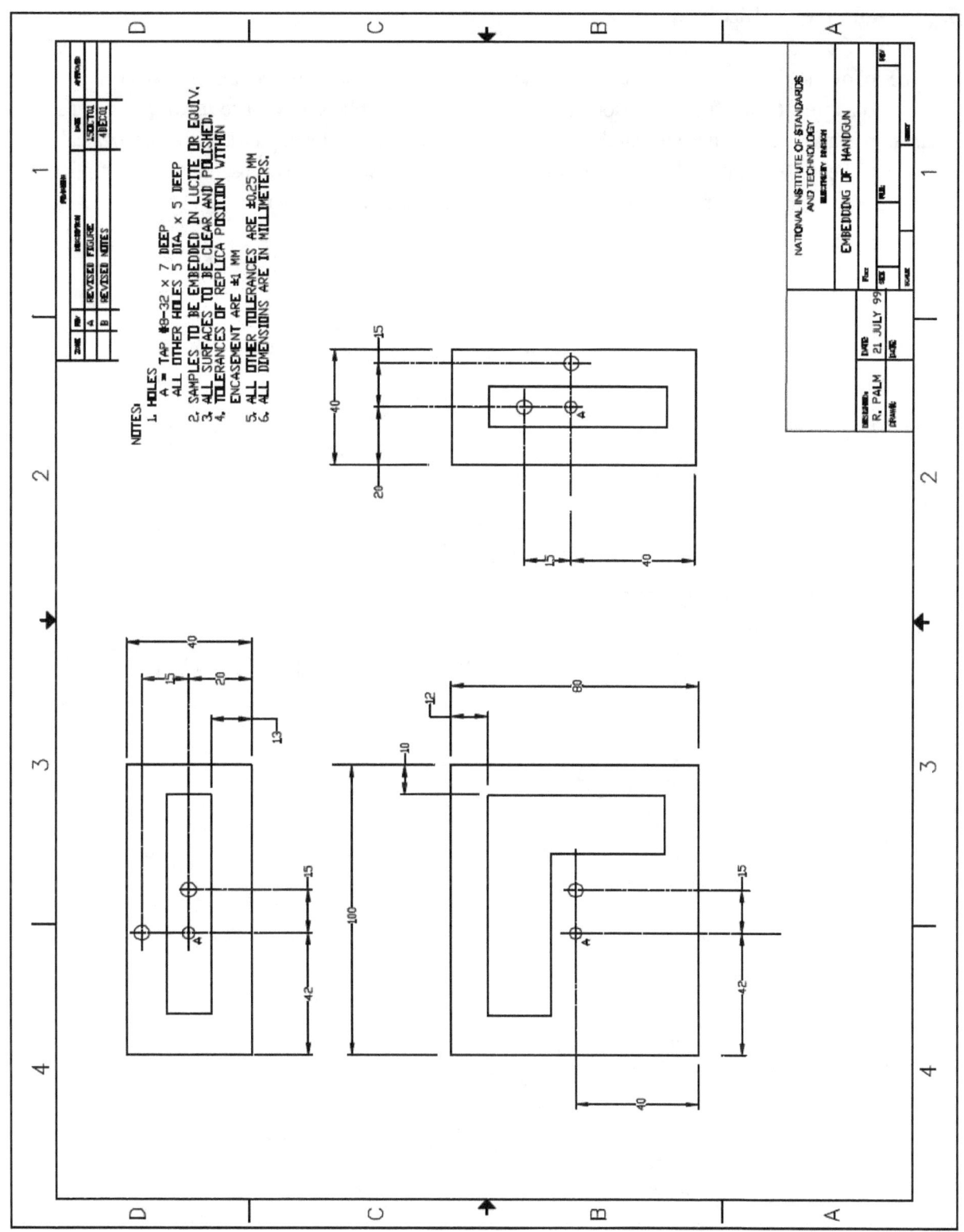

5.2 Medium Object Size Test Objects

The following mechanical drawings are of the replica of the *medium object size* item that is considered a threat to an officer, a prisoner, an inmate, and the public safety. The *medium object size* threat item is a knife. The mechanical drawings are arranged in the following order: the mechanical drawing of the replica of the knife and the location of the replica within the encasement. Two replicas are made and encased, one from each of the materials indicated in the drawings.

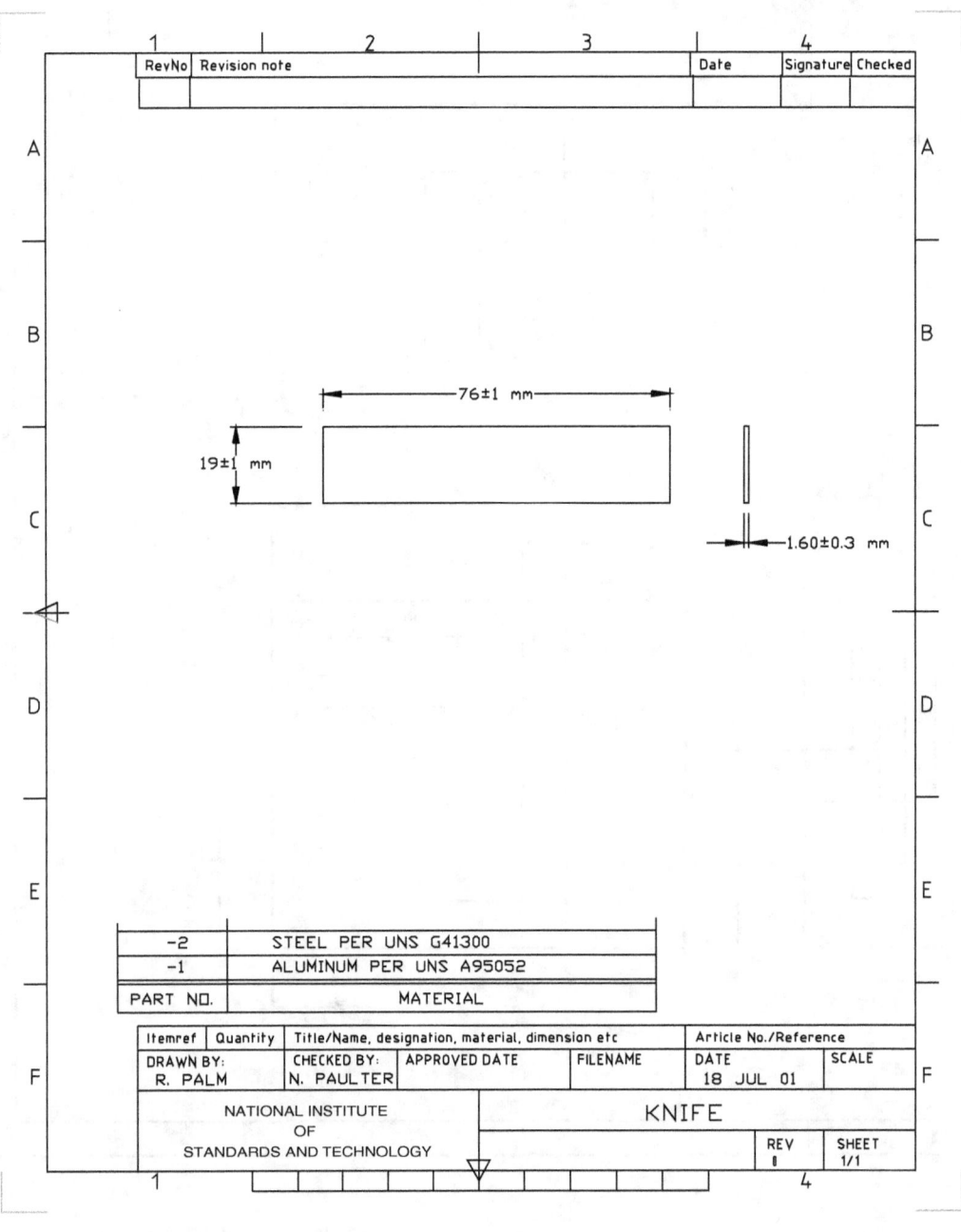

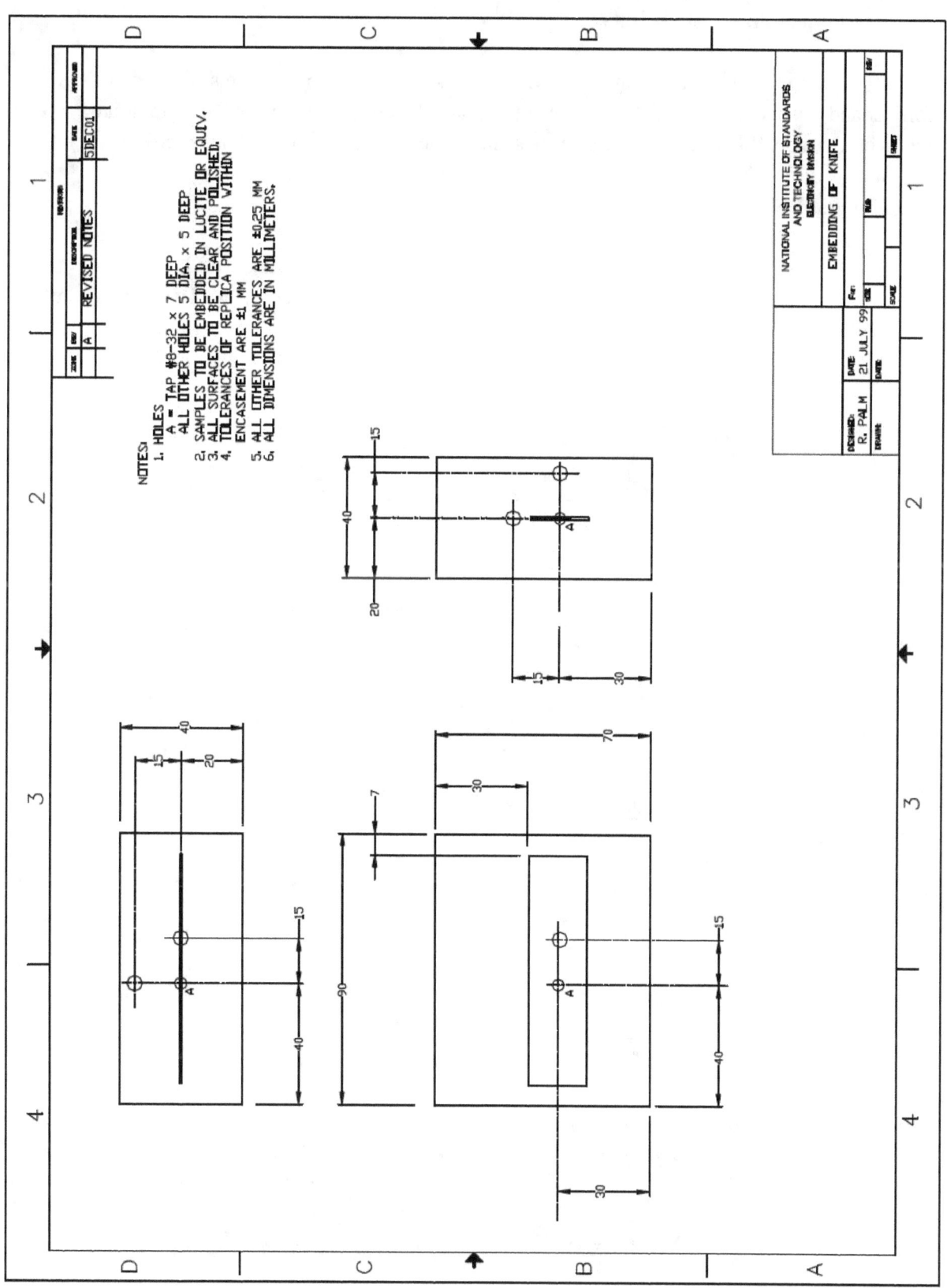

5.3 Small Object Size Test Objects

The following mechanical drawings are replicas of the small hard-to-find items considered a threat to officer and prisoner safety and that can be used to defeat security measures. These items are replicas of: a handcuff key, a nonferromagnetic stainless steel knife, and a #2 Phillips screwdriver bit.

5.3.1 Handcuff Key

This section contains the following mechanical drawings: a replica of a handcuff key, a *small object size test object;* and the location of the *test object* within the encasement. Two replicas are made and encased, one from each of the materials indicated in the drawing.

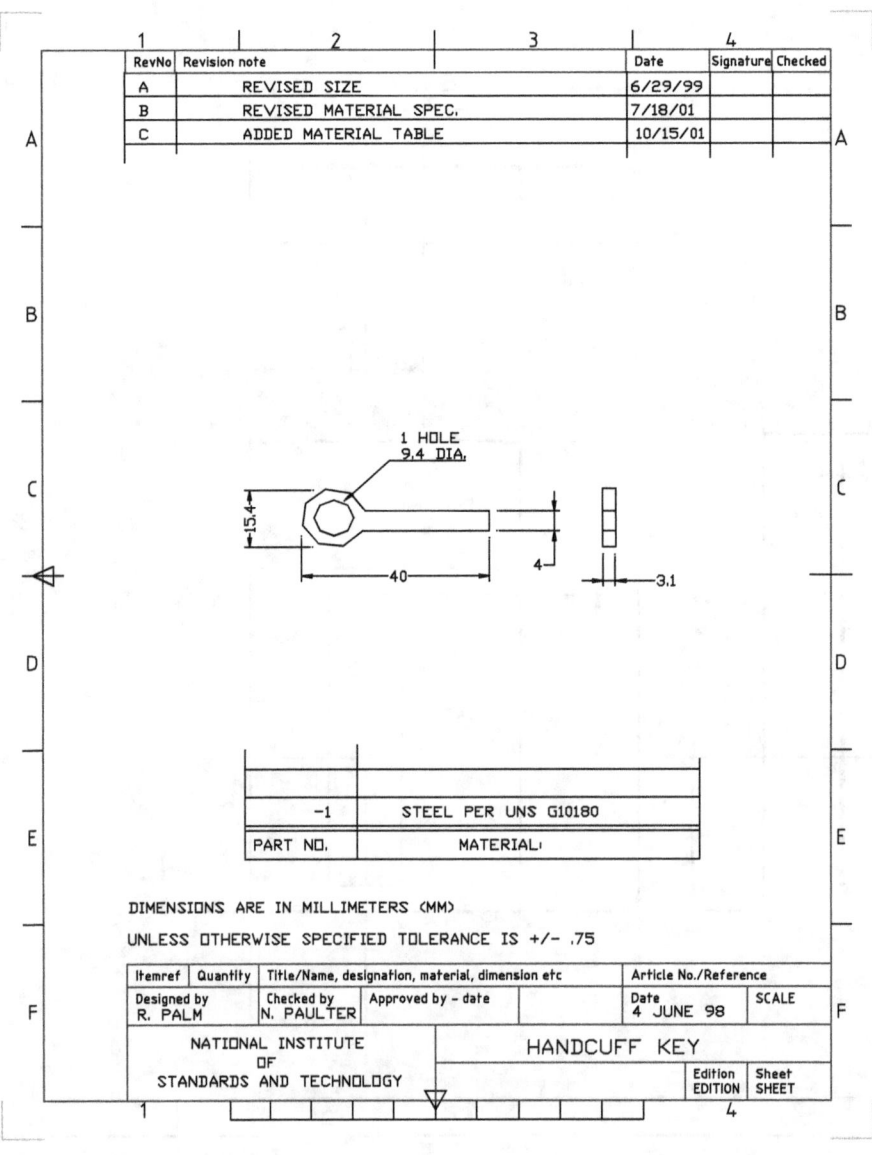

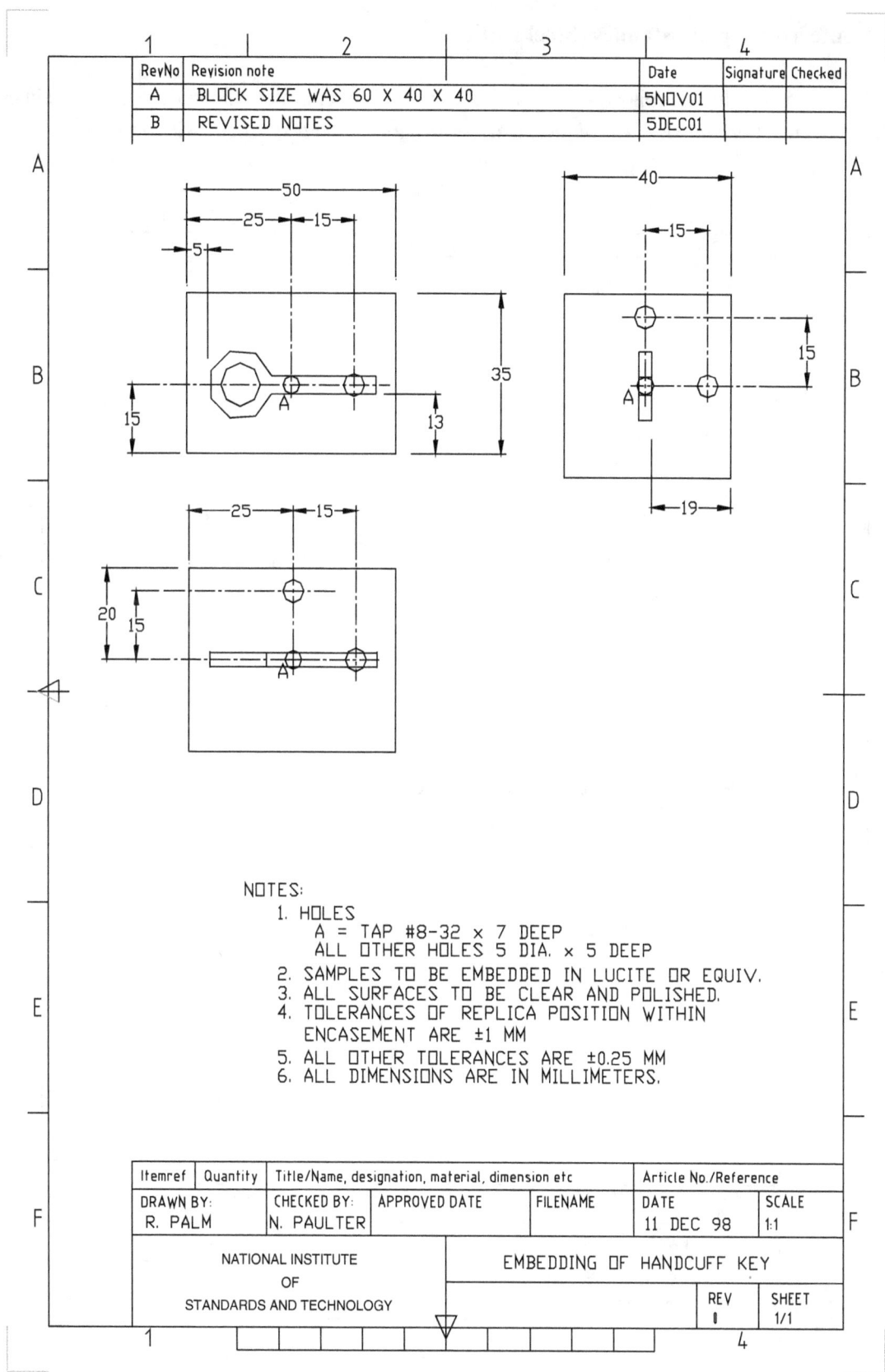

5.3.2 Nonferromagnetic Stainless Steel Knife

This section contains the following mechanical drawings: a replica of a nonferromagnetic stainless steel knife, a *small object size test object;* and the location of the *test object* within the encasement.

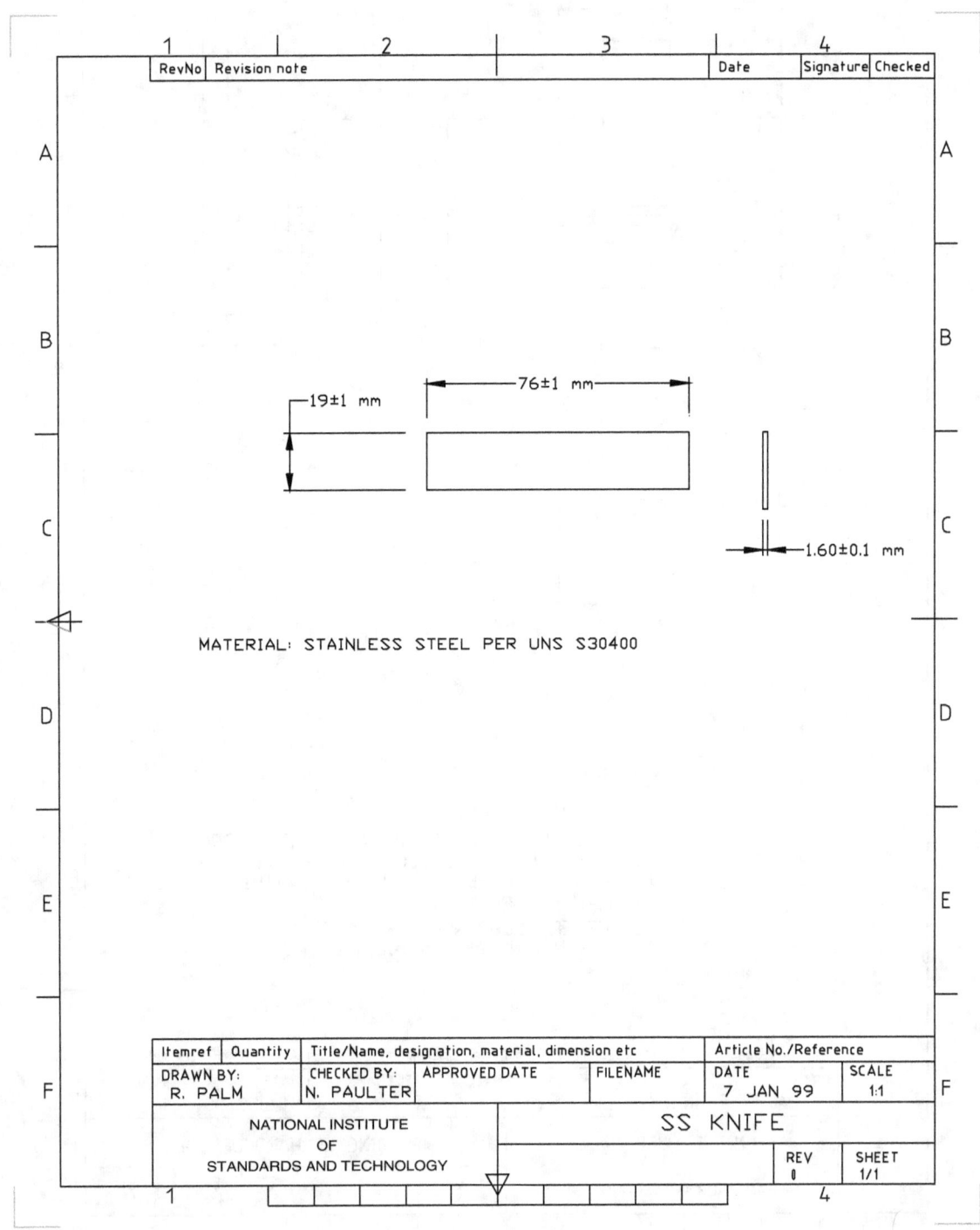

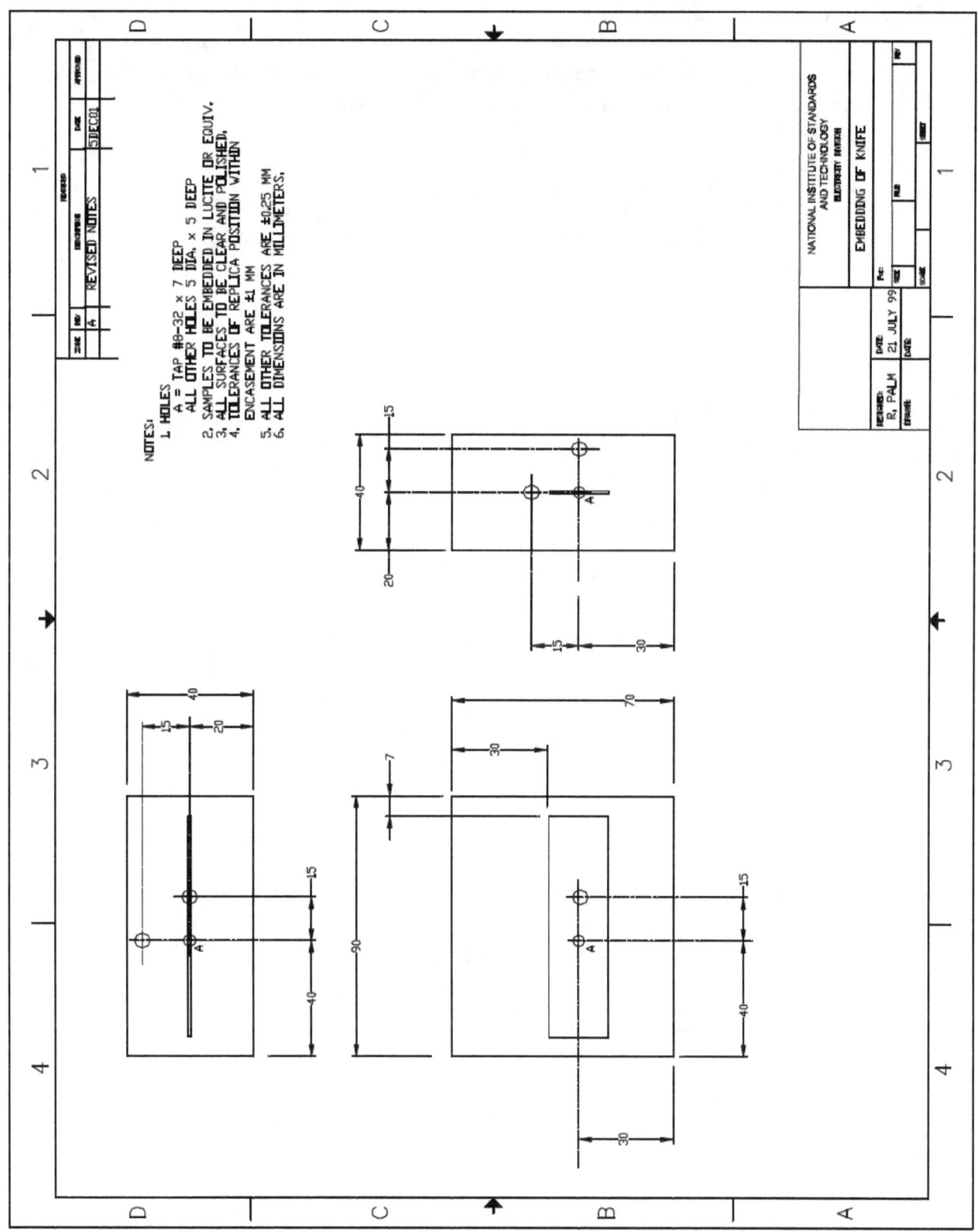

5.3.3 Screwdriver Bit, Phillips, #2

This section contains the following mechanical drawings: a replica of a #2 Phillips screwdriver bit, a *small object size test object*; and the location of the *test object* within the encasement.

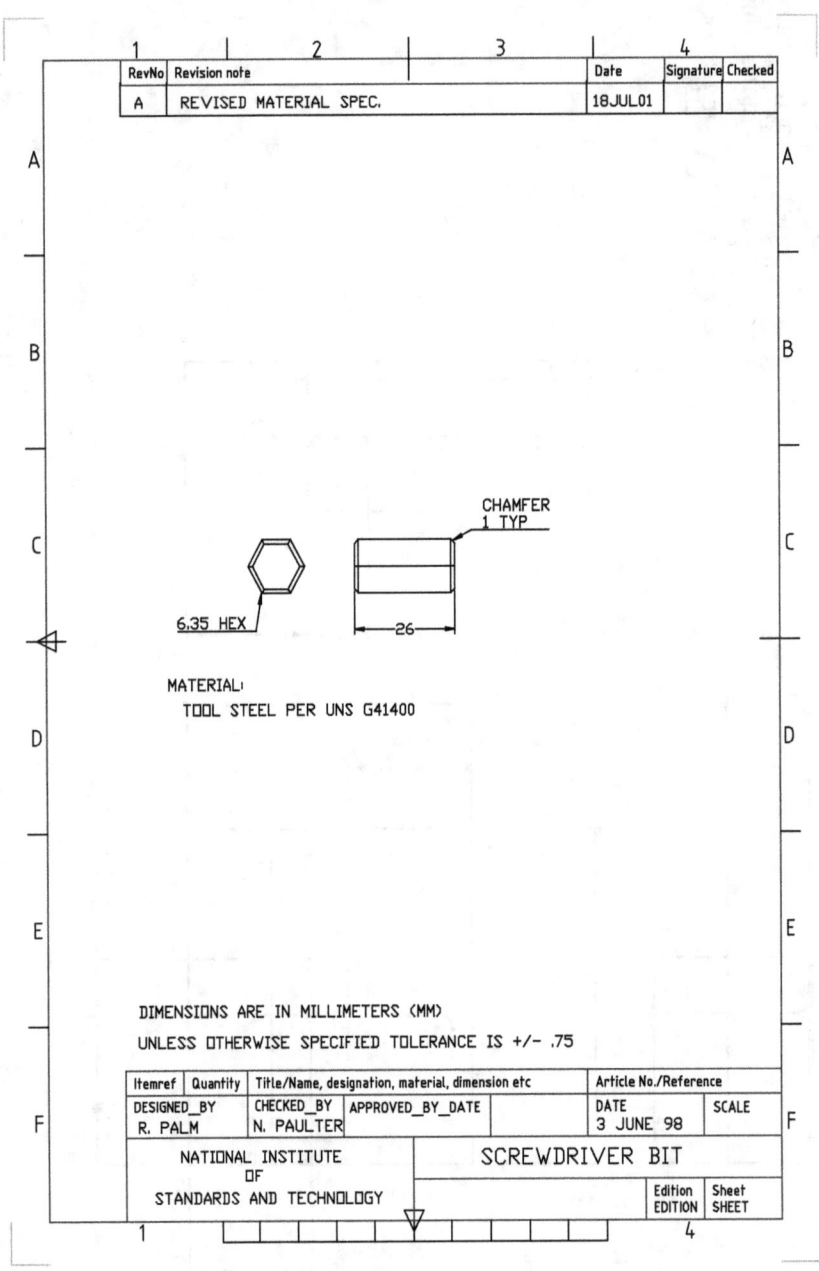

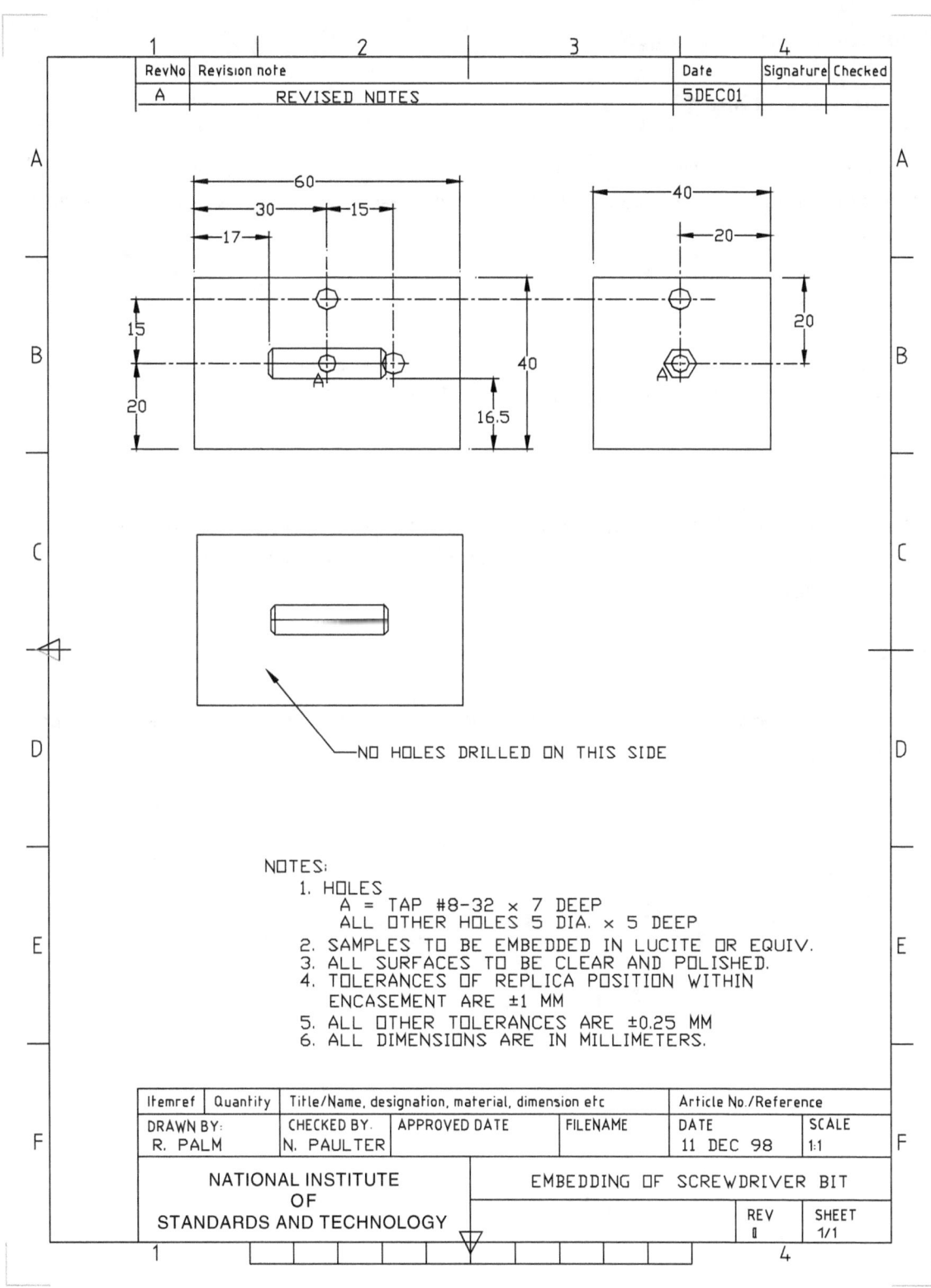

5.4 Innocuous Item Test Objects

5.4.1 Large Object Size

The *innocuous item test objects* for the *large object size* detector classification are the set of coins and the replicas of a set of coins, a belt buckle, eyeglasses, a key ring with keys, a cigarette pack, and a watch.

5.4.1.1 Set of Coins

The set of coins shall consist of two each United States (U.S.) pennies, U.S. nickels, U.S. dimes, and U.S. quarters minted between the years 1990 and 2000.

5.4.1.2 Belt Buckle

The replica of the belt buckle, an *innocuous item test object*, shall be made from a rod of stainless steel, classification UNS S30400, having a diameter of 6.4 mm ± 0.4 mm, and bending into a circle with an inside diameter of 50 mm ± 5 mm.

5.4.1.3 Eyeglasses

The following provides the mechanical drawings for the replica of the eyeglasses, an *innocuous item test object*.

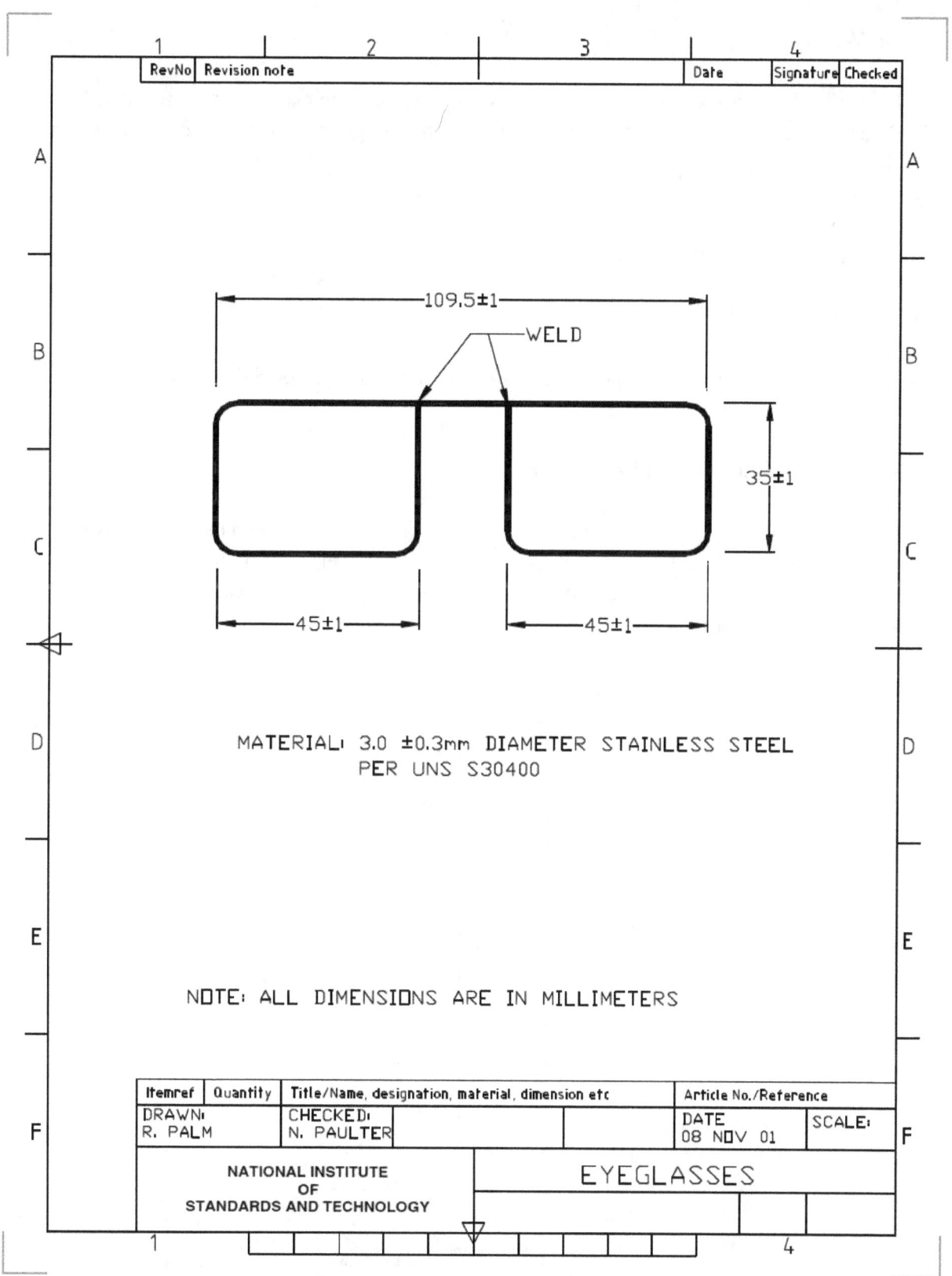

5.4.1.4 Watch

The replica of the watch, an *innocuous item test object*, shall be made from a disc-shaped object. The following provides the physical dimensions and material designation for the replica of the watch:

    diameter: 30 mm ± 5 mm
    thickness: 5 mm ± 1 mm
    material: UNS S30400.

5.4.2 Medium Object Size

The *innocuous item test objects* for the *medium object size* detector classification are the replicas of the eyeglasses and the belt buckle.

5.4.3 Innocuous Item Test Object Holder

The first drawing shows the location of the *innocuous item test objects* on the *innocuous item test object* holder, and the subsequent mechanical drawings are of the parts of the *innocuous item test object* holder and its assembly. All components of the holder shall be constructed of nonelectrically conductive and nonmagnetic materials.

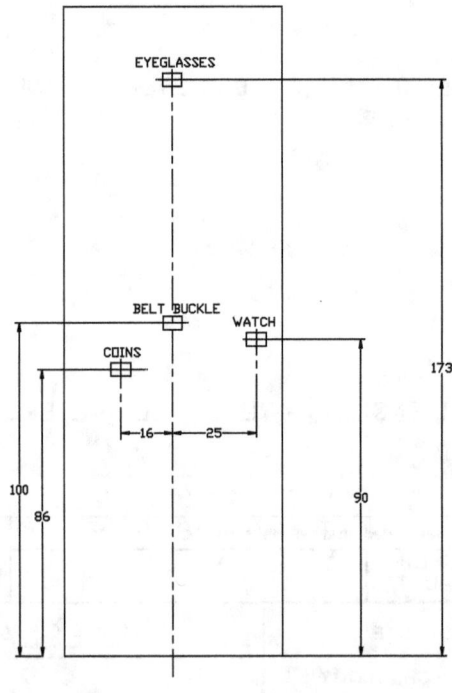

NOTE: ALL DIMENSIONS ARE IN CENTIMETERS.
TOLERANCE FOR ALL DIMENSIONS IS ±2 CENTIMETERS.

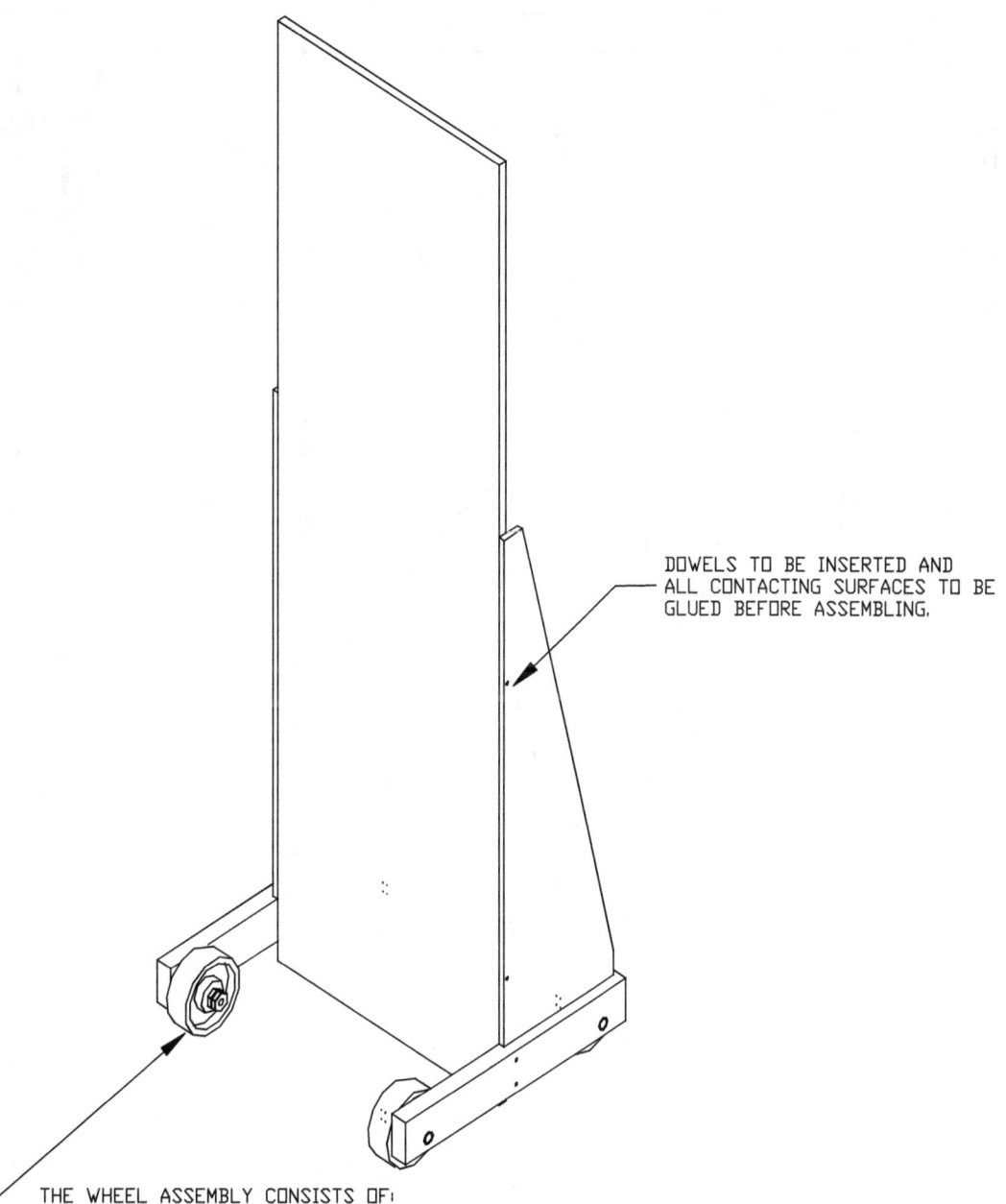

DOWELS TO BE INSERTED AND ALL CONTACTING SURFACES TO BE GLUED BEFORE ASSEMBLING.

THE WHEEL ASSEMBLY CONSISTS OF:
BOLT (HEX HEAD, 1/2-13, 10CM LONG, NYLON) INSERTED THRU IN THE FOLLOWING ORDER:
WHEEL AND SIDE MOUNT (SEE DWG. NO. 2001C1105)
WASHER #1 (SIZE 1/2, NYLON)
WHEEL (15 CM ±2 CM DIA, 4 CM ±1 CM WIDE, 1.27 CM ±0.1CM AXLE HOLE, POLYOLEFIN)
WASHER #2 (SAME AS WASHER #1)
NUT #1 (1/2-13, NYLON)
JAM NUT (SAME AS NUT #1).

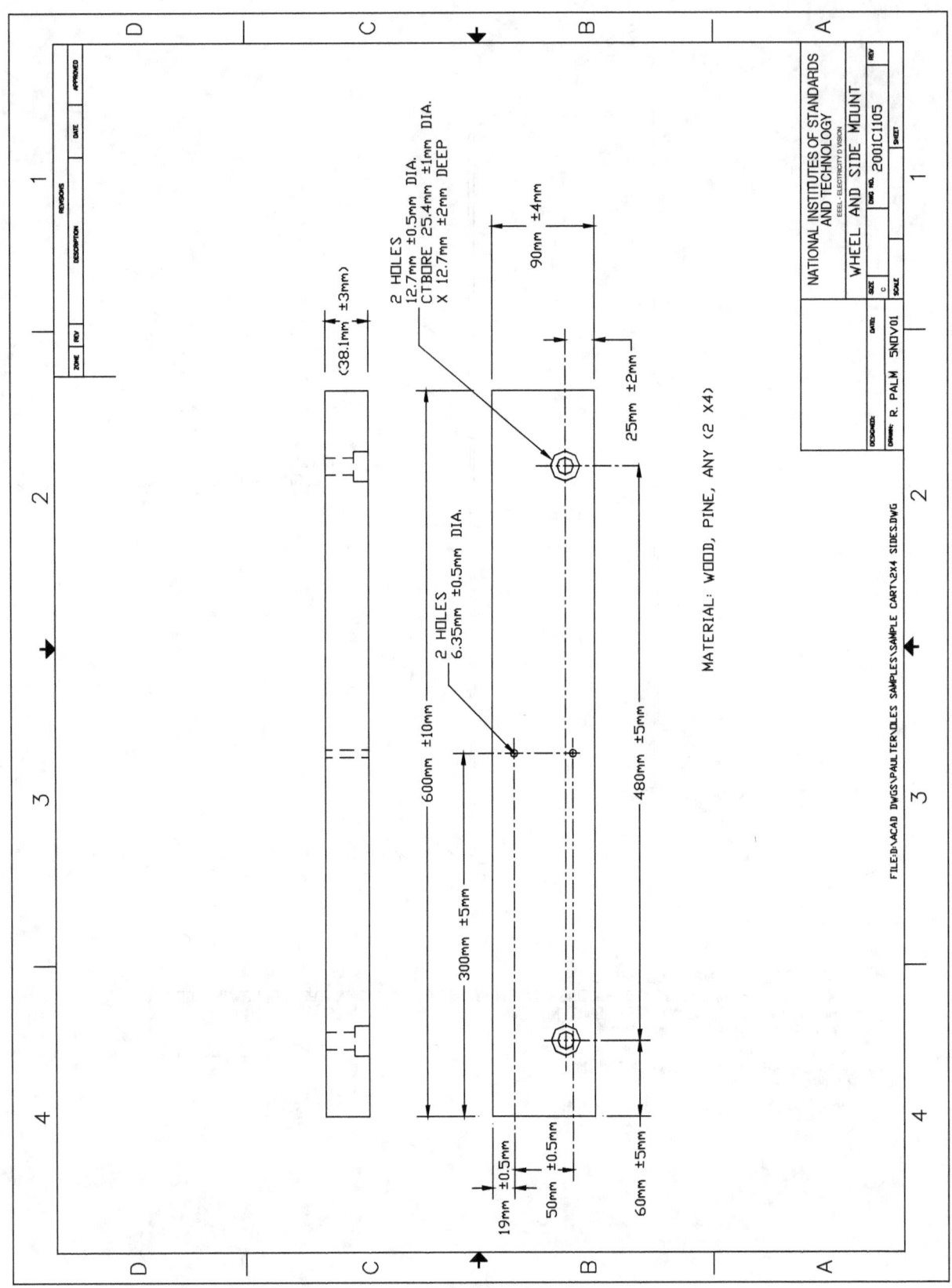

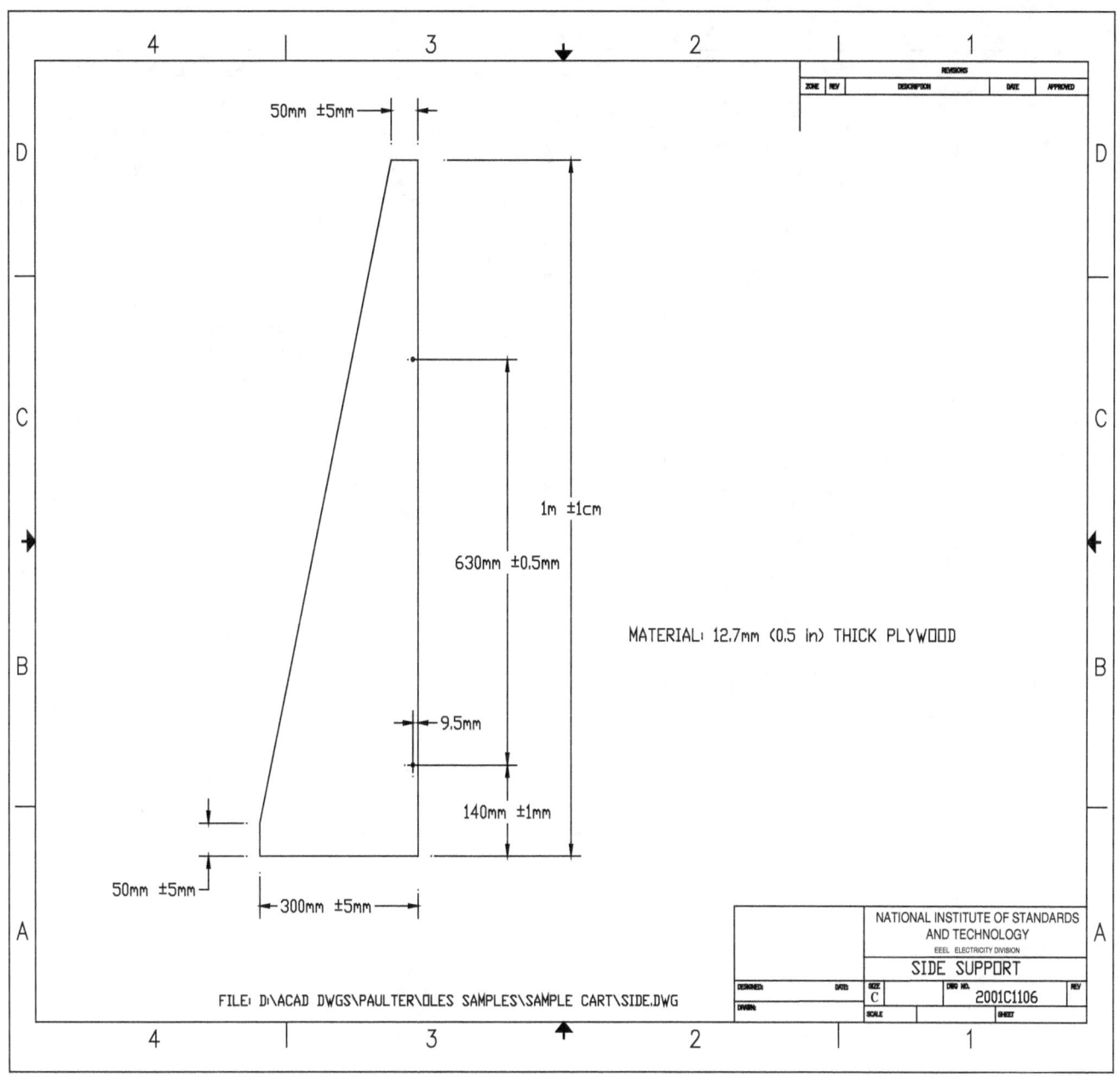

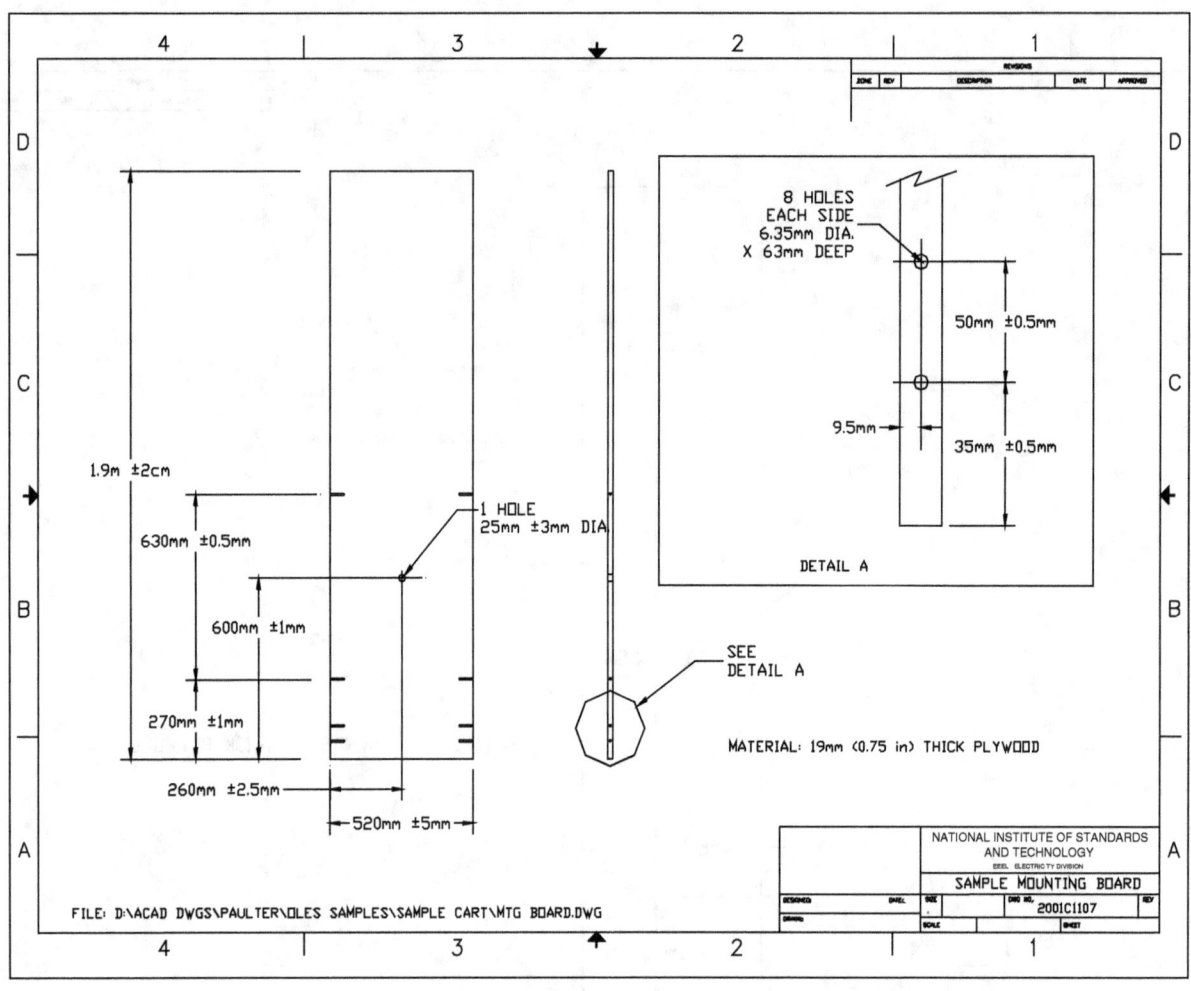

6. COMPLIANCE TEST REPORT FORM

The Compliance Test Report (CTR) form shall be used in conjunction with NIJ Standard–0601.02, *Walk-Through Metal Detectors for Use in Concealed Weapon and Contraband Detection*, and shall become a part of the official records of the compliance testing of each metal detector model submitted for testing. All sections of the form shall be completed.

An electronic file of the report form is available from the NLECTC Compliance Testing Office, National Law Enforcement and Corrections Technology Center-National (NLECTC-National). Requests for this file can be sent to: NLECTC-National, Attn: Metal Detector Testing Program, P.O. Box 1160, Rockville, MD 20849–1160; or to the E-mail address, **asknlectc@nlectc.org**.

7. REFERENCES

The following normative documents contain provisions, which through reference in this text, constitute provisions of this Standards Publication. By reference herein these publications are adopted, in whole or in part, as indicated.

ACGIH–0302 (1996), American Conference of Governmental Industrial Hygienists, *Documentation of the Threshold Limit Values, Sub-Radio Frequency (30 kHz and below) Magnetic Fields.*

ANSI S1.4, 1971, American National Standards Institute, *Specifications for General Purpose Sound Level Meters.*

ASTM Designation F 1468–95, Section 13, American Society for Testing and Materials, *Standard Practice for Evaluation of Metallic Weapons Detectors for Controlled Access Search and Screening, Section 13, Procedure for Testing for Outside Influences: Electrical.*

EN 50081–1 1992, European Standard, *Electromagnetic Compatibility - Generic Emission Standard, Part 1: Residential, Commercial, and Light Industry.*

EN 50082–1 1998, European Standard, *Electromagnetic Compatibility - Generic Immunity Standard, Part 1: Residential, Commercial, and Light Industry.*

IEC 68–2–27 1987, International Electrotechnical Commission, *Basic Environmental Testing Procedures, Part 2: Tests - Test Ea and Guidance: Shock.*

IEC 68–2–29 1987, International Electrotechnical Commission, *Basic Environmental Testing Procedures, Part 2: Tests - Test Eb and Guidance: Bump.*

IEC 60529 2001–2, International Electrotechnical Commission, *Degrees of Protection Provided by Enclosures (IP Code).*

IEEE C95.1–1991, Institute of Electrical and Electronic Engineers, *Standard for Safety Levels with Respect to Human Exposure to Radio Frequency Electromagnetic Fields, 3 kHz to 300 GHz.*

ISO 9001:2000, International Organization for Standardization 9001, *Quality Systems - Model for Quality Assurance in Design, Development, Production, Installation and Servicing.*

ISO 10012–1:1993–01–15, International Standards Organization, *Quality Assurance Requirements for Measuring Equipment, Part 1: Metrological Confirmation System for Measuring Equipment.*

ISO 10012–2:1997–09–15, International Standards Organization, *Quality Assurance for Measuring Equipment, Part 2: Guidelines for control measurement process.*

ISO 17025:1999–12–15, International Standards Organization, *General Requirements for the Competence of Testing and Calibration Laboratories.*

MIL–STD–461E Method RS101, Military Standard, *Requirements for the Control of Electromagnetic Interference Characteristics of Subsystems and Equipment, Method RS101, Radiated Susceptibility, Magnetic Field, 30 Hz to 100 kHz.*

MIL–STD–810F Method 501.4, Military Standard, *Test Method Standard for Environmental Engineering Considerations and Laboratory Tests, Method 501.4, High Temperature.*

MIL–STD–810F Method 502.4, Military Standard, *Test Method Standard for Environmental Engineering Considerations and Laboratory Tests, Method 502.4, Low Temperature.*

MIL–STD–810F Method 505.4, Military Standard, *Test Method Standard for Environmental Engineering Considerations and Laboratory Tests, Method 505.4, Solar Radiation (Sunshine).*

MIL–STD–810F Method 507.4, Military Standard, *Test Method Standard for Environmental Engineering Considerations and Laboratory Tests, Method 507.4, Humidity.*

MIL–STD–810F Method 509.4, Military Standard, *Test Method Standard for Environmental Engineering Considerations and Laboratory Tests, Method 509.4, Salt Fog.*

NIJ, National Institute of Justice, *A Users' Guide for Hand-Held and Walk-Through Metal Weapon Detectors*, 2000.

NIST Technical Note 1297, *Guidelines for evaluating and expressing the uncertainty of NIST measurement results*, U.S. Dept. of Commerce, 1994.

Safety Code, Recommended Safety Procedures for the Selection, Installation and Use of Active Metal Detectors, Radiation Protection Bureau, Canadian Minister of National Health and Welfare.

UL 60950, Underwriters Laboratories, *Safety for Information Technology Equipment*.

About the Law Enforcement and Corrections Standards and Testing Program

The Law Enforcement and Corrections Standards and Testing Program is sponsored by the Office of Science and Technology of the National Institute of Justice (NIJ), U.S. Department of Justice. The program responds to the mandate of the Justice System Improvement Act of 1979, which directed NIJ to encourage research and development to improve the criminal justice system and to disseminate the results to Federal, State, and local agencies.

The Law Enforcement and Corrections Standards and Testing Program is an applied research effort that determines the technological needs of justice system agencies, sets minimum performance standards for specific devices, tests commercially available equipment against those standards, and disseminates the standards and the test results to criminal justice agencies nationally and internationally.

The program operates through:

The *Law Enforcement and Corrections Technology Advisory Council* (LECTAC), consisting of nationally recognized criminal justice practitioners from Federal, State, and local agencies, which assesses technological needs and sets priorities for research programs and items to be evaluated and tested.

The *Office of Law Enforcement Standards* (OLES) at the National Institute of Standards and Technology, which develops voluntary national performance standards for compliance testing to ensure that individual items of equipment are suitable for use by criminal justice agencies. The standards are based upon laboratory testing and evaluation of representative samples of each item of equipment to determine the key attributes, develop test methods, and establish minimum performance requirements for each essential attribute. In addition to the highly technical standards, OLES also produces technical reports and user guidelines that explain in nontechnical terms the capabilities of available equipment.

The *National Law Enforcement and Corrections Technology Center* (NLECTC), operated by a grantee, which supervises a national compliance testing program conducted by independent laboratories. The standards developed by OLES serve as performance benchmarks against which commercial equipment is measured. The facilities, personnel, and testing capabilities of the independent laboratories are evaluated by OLES prior to testing each item of equipment, and OLES helps the NLECTC staff review and analyze data. Test results are published in Equipment Performance Reports designed to help justice system procurement officials make informed purchasing decisions.

Publications are available at no charge through the National Law Enforcement and Corrections Technology Center. Some documents are also available online through the Internet/World Wide Web. To request a document or additional information, call 800–248–2742 or 301–519–5060, or write:

> National Law Enforcement and Corrections Technology Center
> P.O. Box 1160
> Rockville, MD 20849–1160
> E-Mail: asknlectc@nlectc.org
> World Wide Web address: http://www.nlectc.org

This document is not intended to create, does not create, and may not be relied upon to create any rights, substantive or procedural, enforceable at law by any party in any matter civil or criminal.

Opinions or points of view expressed in this document represent a consensus of the authors and do not represent the official position or policies of the U.S. Department of Justice. The products and manufacturers discussed in this document are presented for informational purposes only and do not constitute product approval or endorsement by the U.S. Department of Justice.

The National Institute of Justice is a component of the Office of Justice Programs, which also includes the Bureau of Justice Assistance, the Bureau of Justice Statistics, the Office of Juvenile Justice and Delinquency Prevention, and the Office for Victims of Crime.

www.ingramcontent.com/pod-product-compliance
Lightning Source LLC
Chambersburg PA
CBHW081855170526
45167CB00007B/3029